'As a former pro surfer, tr [barcode] of my career, and in this next stage of my life Rod has helped me to transition to where I want to be for the future. I want to be ripping in my sixties!' – **Joel Parkinson, professional surfer and world champion**

'Training with Rod changed my life. I thought I understood fitness and my body until I walked into his classroom. Rod linked my own knowledge with nutrition insights and correct training methods. He's also taken my patience, accountability and awareness to a whole new level. It's like having a superpower I never thought I could own! I am now at peace with myself and cannot wait to take on the next challenge. Bring on the future!' – **Harry Bink, professional freestyle motocross rider and X Games medallist**

'Rod's coaching has been nothing but life-changing. I've learned to train smarter and be more holistic in my approach to move-ment and daily habits. He's elevated my skills and character to a whole new level. I want to be active across all my sports until I'm 100. Anything is possible with the methods and mindset he teaches.' – **Alex Hayes, artist, action sports athlete and social media influencer**

'I trained with Rod in the latter half of my surfing career. I only wish I had worked with him sooner. I saw a drastic improvement in my surfing performance through implementing the Holistica Movement in my everyday life. While working with Rod, I won my first World Qualifying Series event and qualified for the WCT for the second time. The movements I learned are still part of my daily routine.' – **Ricardo Christie, professional surfer**

'I love working with Rod because I have seen a big improvement in my balance and stability, which has helped me a lot with my skateboarding. The types of movements and exercises Rod teaches are all different, and I'm heaps stronger in places like my core and hips, and I'm stronger in my mind.' – **Chloe Cavell, professional skateboarder and Olympian**

'I was introduced to Rod's work a few years ago when I had the opportunity to train with him in Australia – it was one of the best training experiences I've had. I've added his mobility methods to my routine, because it's a type of training we often leave behind when we prioritise only strength.' – **Marcus 'Buchecha' Almeida, 13-time Brazilian jiu-jitsu black-belt world champion**

'Rod has not only helped my body evolve, but he has been a great mentor. Rod's coaching is world class and easily adaptable for all different levels and personal goals. I take these lessons with me everywhere I go. His vast knowledge and experience have helped my overall body movement, strength and awareness.' – **Thalison Soares, Brazilian jiu-jitsu black-belt world champion**

'My introduction to Rod's training methods at the early age of sixteen allowed me to create a solid foundation of fitness, one that has helped me prevent injuries, all while pursuing a daily routine of surfing and training. His holistic approach to fitness and wellbeing has inspired me, among many others, to seek my highest potential in any facet of life.' – **Thomas Carvalho, professional surfer**

Rodrigo Perez is a professional coach and founder of Holistic Pro Health Performance. For over two decades, he has coached and trained countless elite performers and world champions, through to the everyday athlete wanting to increase their mobility, motivation and healthy habits. With a degree in Exercise Science, his movement methodology and holistic longevity and wellness approach have helped thousands of people become more aware of their bodies, improve their nutrition, break through plateaus in their performance and ultimately become the optimal version of themselves.

Erin,
Big Congratulations
for massive Performance
in Australia. well Done.

THE ART OF
LONGEVITY

YOUR PRACTICAL GUIDE TO TOTAL
MIND AND BODY WELLNESS

I Hope you enjoy the Read.

RODRIGO PEREZ

14/05/2024

PENGUIN BOOKS

UK | USA | Canada | Ireland | Australia
India | New Zealand | South Africa | China

Penguin Books is part of the Penguin Random House group of companies whose addresses can be found at global.penguinrandomhouse.com.

Penguin
Random House
Australia

First published by Penguin Books, 2024

Text copyright © Rodrigo Perez, 2024

Photography copyright © Rodrigo Perez/Holistic Pro Health Performance, 2024

The moral right of the author has been asserted.

Cover design by Alex Ross Creative © Penguin Random House Australia Pty Ltd
Cover Images: woman surfing by Getty Images / Konstantin Trubavin; Rod Perez by Bruno Martinez @brunoomartinez (front) and Jackson O'Brien @jacksonobrien_ (back)
Internal design by Post Pre-press Group, Brisbane
Internal photography by Rodrigo Ximenes @friction_free
Typeset in 12/18.8 pt Adobe Caslon Pro by Post Pre-press Group, Brisbane

Printed and bound in Australia by Griffin Press, an accredited ISO AS/NZ 14001 Environmental Management Systems printer.

A catalogue record for this book is available from the National Library of Australia

ISBN 978 1 76104 992 7

penguin.com.au

MIX
Paper | Supporting
responsible forestry
FSC® C018684

We at Penguin Random House Australia acknowledge that Aboriginal and Torres Strait Islander peoples are the first storytellers and Traditional Custodians of the land on which we live and work. We honour Aboriginal and Torres Strait Islander peoples' continuous connection to Country, waters, skies and communities. We celebrate Aboriginal and Torres Strait Islander stories, traditions and living cultures; and we pay our respects to Elders past and present.

To my beloved mother,

*You've moved on to a different world, but the love, strength,
inspiration and lessons you provided remain right here with me.
Your unwavering belief in me and your many sacrifices have inspired
and fuelled my determination to work hard and achieve my dreams.
I dedicate every page in this book to you. Your legacy lives on in
everything I've achieved and the priceless treasures I've gathered along
the way. Thank you for being my guiding light, my true rock.*

With all my love and gratitude,

Rod B. Perez

'*When your vibe is your tribe, it's so obvious!* Rod came into my life at a time when I was seeking to evolve healthy habits as I aged. His natural attention to detail, unwavering curiosity and deep love for witnessing nature's healing paths, expressed through his clients, is powerfully infectious. It's been an honour to partner with Rod for our Art of Longevity workshops and retreats. We've joined our complimentary knowledge base with simple, practical applications and teachings to create a fun, open atmosphere that enhances the connection between mind, body and spirit for all involved.'

Tom Carroll, two-time world surf champion, three-time Pipe Masters champion, and all-around Australian legend

CONTENTS

INTRODUCTION: MY STORY: HOW I GOT INTO
HEALTHY LIVING AND LONGEVITY   1

   My spine   2

   My lovely mum   6

   The bacteria   8

   My methodology   11

1. THE IMPORTANCE OF ESTABLISHING A ROUTINE   15

   Cognitive health: staying sharp   20

2. CREATING A NEW ROUTINE THAT WORKS FOR YOU   25

   How consistency can benefit your health and longevity   26

   The morning routine ritual   31

   The importance of focus when it comes to routine   36

   Discipline gives you direction   38

   The importance of direction in achieving your goals   39

   Start each day with a wake-up routine   41

   MORNING ROUTINE   44

   NIGHT ROUTINE   59

3. MOVE WELL, MOVE STRONGER AND MOVE FOR LIFE!   65

   What is mobility?   70

   The importance of mobility   72

The hip joint and hip mobility 74

Free hips = free flow – Graham's story 76

Let's get stable (stability training) 77

Is there a difference between stretching and mobility? 80

Core work – let's be supple for life 80

The key points for a good core program 84

Cardiovascular training 85

Smart cardio 85

Using endurance to achieve durability 88

Pure strength 90

THE 12-WEEK TRAINING PROGRAM 92

12-WEEK PROGRAM, PHASE 1 108

12-WEEK PROGRAM, PHASE 2 130

12-WEEK PROGRAM, PHASE 3 146

4. NOURISH YOUR BODY 162

Prioritise nutrient-dense foods 163

Hydrate, hydrate, hydrate 163

Don't fear fats 163

Mind your microbiome 164

Balance your macronutrients 164

One per cent improvement each day – no excuses! 171

The importance of hydration and gut health 176

Alcohol 179

Gut health 181

Four healthy gut diets (paleo, Mediterranean,
    plant-based and keto) 185

Intermittent fasting 192

What your average day will look like   197

My go-to daily routine   198

The morning routine: seven pillars for a better life   201

SMOOTHIE RECIPES   202

BREAKFAST RECIPES   205

LUNCH RECIPES   208

DINNER RECIPES   212

SNACKS   216

5.   ENERGISE AND REFRESH – THE IMPORTANCE OF BREATHING   218

Diaphragmatic breathing   223

How to practise diaphragmatic breathing   224

Nasal breathing   227

Breathe safely, efficiently and properly   229

The power of 'box breathing': unlocking your potential   233

6.   MEDITATION – BE AT PEACE, GET IN THE ZONE (WITH TOM CARROLL)   236

Why should I meditate every day?   240

The benefits of meditation   244

Being 'in the zone' – achieving a 'flow state'   247

Tom Carroll's story   251

7.   CONNECTING TO THE ENVIRONMENT AROUND YOU   258

The importance of connecting with the environment for athletes   263

How nature helps your wellbeing   264

Practising appreciation and gratitude   266

8. COMMITTING TO RECOVERY   274

Acknowledge the importance of recovery   276

Create a recovery plan   276

Keep track of your progress   277

Stay positive and be compassionate with yourself   277

Seek help when you need to   278

Massage therapy   279

Sauna therapy   282

Ice bath recovery   284

Hyperbaric oxygen therapy   285

PEMF therapy   288

Peptides   290

Platelet-rich plasma   290

Stem cell therapy   291

Combining therapies   291

The 'optimal' view of recovery   292

9. THE ART OF LONGEVITY –
MAKING THE CONNECTION   295

Cut out the bad habits where we can

and be open to learning new ones   296

Understanding your authenticity   308

Trust and respect the process: longevity is our goal   310

10. THE SAMURAI WAY   311

Bringing the samurai way into your life   312

The art of self-control   316

The power of change over the long haul   319

ACKNOWLEDGEMENTS   323

INTRODUCTION

MY STORY: HOW I GOT INTO HEALTHY LIVING AND LONGEVITY

Like most people, I've had my fair share of health issues. When I was a kid growing up in Brazil, I couldn't play sports like my friends. I had bronchitis and had trouble breathing – whenever I tried to exercise, I quickly became short of breath and my heart started pounding. I'd only last ten minutes playing soccer or basketball, skateboarding, doing karate or kung fu. It was frustrating and I became really disappointed with my limitations. Soon I started putting myself down.

I knew something was wrong, but I didn't know what to do. And with each passing year, because I couldn't exercise, I started putting on weight. My mum did everything she could, but she didn't have much medical or dietary knowledge. The doctors prescribed me anti-inflammatory medications and antibiotics for my bronchitis, but they didn't really help. They actually seemed to make it *worse*. As my metabolism slowed, my weight increased even more, and I started losing muscle.

As a kid from a low–middle socio-economic background,

we didn't have a lot of money, but I was lucky enough to meet a great doctor who sent me off to see a group of researchers who were working with kids with similar respiratory problems. They recommended certain physical exercises as well as swimming to 'open up' our breathing pathways, increase our lung capacity, improve our overall health and address other associated health problems that might develop over time.

This was a big challenge for me because I had to learn to breathe properly, maintain a good rhythm while swimming and keep my heart rate steady. In time, swimming helped clear my lungs, and allowed me to live the life of a normal kid. After a year or so of hard work, my bronchitis was gone! I couldn't believe it. From there, I developed new habits and training principles. The results were infectious; I was fast becoming a new person. I learned everything I could about exercise, health, the role of the mind, the philosophies behind martial arts and more. But as we all know, when you become a teenager, things can easily fall apart again.

MY SPINE

I started bodyboarding when I was around 16 years old. Before then the ocean was only a thing to dream about: the beaches were far from home, I was a city boy. When I got to university and had my driver's licence, things started to change – I wanted to learn to surf. I wanted to live and breathe its culture. I had it in my mind to move to California or Australia, but I chose Australia because I was already living vicariously through the photos of beautiful stretches of beaches and waves that I saw in surf magazines.

I remember ads saying, 'Come to Australia! Learn to surf! Learn English!' Unfortunately, my parents never had money to send me, but I worked hard in my last year of university, saved and made my surf lifestyle dream come true.

In the middle of 2004, at the age of 27, having lived in Australia for several years, I decided to go travelling. I wound up in London and was pounding the pavement, looking everywhere for a job, trying to make ends meet. One morning I woke up and – *boom* – I felt a pain in my back so intense that it knocked me out. I had never experienced anything like it before, right in the middle of my back, in the thoracic area. It was hard to do anything – work, train, socialise. I couldn't even breathe properly. The pain was strong and persistent, and no amount of stretching or exercise could relieve it – or take the edge off my frustration. I decided to slow down and rest. I would keep doing some gentle stretching routines and I added some therapeutic massage. After three months or so I started to see some improvement, but I knew my condition was far from fixed. The pain had dulled but the root of the problem hadn't gone away – and was still a bit of a mystery.

At the beginning of 2006, I returned to Australia to start the life that I had dreamed of when I first arrived from Brazil, in the place I now call home: the Gold Coast. I was studying and working three different jobs to save enough money to get my permanent resident visa and pay all the course tuition and licence fees I needed in order to practise as a personal trainer. (I already had a degree from university in Brazil in Exercise Science with a specialisation in Sports Rehabilitation.) At the same time, I was training in Brazilian jiu-jitsu and surfing. A lot! In short,

I was overusing my back muscles, and this was putting pressure on my spine again. That sharp pain was returning, and I was getting down and annoyed because I knew it was related to a bigger problem that had never totally gone away. So I had to ease up on all my training again, but I still had to work to make money, survive, and achieve my goals.

In 2009, I signed a new client – a doctor from an emergency department who was also a Brazilian jiu-jitsu (BJJ) lover. I told him about my own BJJ practice and why I wasn't training as much anymore. I also told him I hated taking painkillers to mask the pain that I knew would soon return.

'Why don't you get an MRI done on your spine?' he suggested.

'Well, I can't – no doctor will give me one,' I said. 'Also, they cost a lot of money, which I don't have.'

'I can help you with a referral,' he replied, 'and we'll find out what's going on with your back.'

I went to a public hospital for the MRI, and four days later I got the results. It didn't look good. I had a unique condition that few physiotherapists, osteopaths and chiropractors had ever seen: a bulging disc between the T5 and T6 vertebrae in the middle of my back between the shoulder blades, and a disc tear between the T6 and T7 vertebrae that was being compressed, becoming inflamed. This was what was causing me all that pain. The majority of cases are found in the cervical area of the neck or around the lower back, but rarely in the thoracic area. The doctor took the results to a spinal surgeon who told me I was a definite candidate for an operation, but that I could also try to treat the pain with some special exercises. I thought to myself, *I'll fix this through exercise and a good diet!*

And so began my research into all the different ways to train the body. I learned which exercises I could use to treat the pain and also improve my spinal function. I ended up learning a lot about body weight training, movement and core stability, and I began to specialise in these areas with my clients. It was an important step, because I also uncovered a wealth of information about diet and other lifestyle factors that are important to overall wellbeing, like the need for sleep and recovery (healing, regaining your strength and allowing your body and mind to reset), and the effects of meditation and breathwork.

Life rolled on – I continued my research, studying more and more cases, always thinking of ways to improve my body and mind with the aim of continuing to do those activities I loved for as long as possible, without limitations, and help others too. Of course, the journey wasn't without its frustrations. There were times when I plateaued, when my training wasn't yielding any results, and when my body wasn't improving.

At this stage, I decided to look into alternative treatments. For one, I found out that my gut wasn't working as it should. I couldn't digest protein properly or absorb its nutrients. On top of that, I had an allergy to dairy and eggs, and I couldn't digest gluten. Actually, I found no shortage of things I had to work on to improve my health and make my body function as it should! I knew that in order to achieve my goals I would have to find the right diet – basically, I needed to completely re-educate myself about food.

So I started spending time with naturopaths. I read all kinds of books about functional medicine, checked out all different types of diets, like the metabolic diet, the blood type diet and countless others. I had blood tests done to see what my body chemistry would respond to. I did an ancestry DNA test and a hormone test and studied how they could potentially influence mood, chemical imbalances, fatigue and more. I will share some of those findings later in the book, including questions that you might consider asking your own health professional.

MY LOVELY MUM

In 2008, doctors found a small cyst in my mum's lung. This was a shock as she'd always seemed so healthy in my eyes and had never been a smoker or a drinker. She was a beautiful Spanish lady who had escaped from Spain at the beginning of World War II with her mum and brother. My grandfather was already in Brazil waiting for them to arrive. The crazy thing, she told me, was that they were meant to travel to Argentina, where people spoke Spanish, but my grandfather had other ideas and sent them to São Paulo. They were so confused when they couldn't understand anyone around them! At the time women couldn't work outside the home; only men could study and have meaningful careers. My mum married my father when she was twenty-five years old and worked very hard in the home her entire life, and later in a bookshop, selling books, pencils, pens and uniforms. Also, she was looking after us and the house. (She has always been my biggest inspiration for her hard work and determination.) But back in 2008, when the doctors found that small cyst, I kept asking myself, *How on Earth did she get lung cancer?*

Looking into her past, I found out that she had contracted the 'white plague' – tuberculosis – back in 1940. Tuberculosis is a serious and infectious bacterial disease that mainly affects the lungs. The treatment was very harsh at the time, and she nearly died. She probably carried some vestige of the illness for many, many years afterwards. She developed high blood pressure from the emotional stress and started to take a heavy dose of medication to regulate it. Always a devoted wife and mother, she was sleeping less and less in order to look after her family. There was never much food around and clean water was scarce, so it was hard to drink the right amount to keep the body properly hydrated. I quickly realised those factors in her early life – compounded by her lifestyle in later life – had increased her chances of developing cancer.

She had surgery to remove the cyst in her lung, but the doctors found another small one on her spine that they didn't want to risk operating on. A year later, that small cyst grew and began to put pressure on her spine, close to her heart. She underwent more surgery, which was now even riskier. She was worried and scared but, as a strong Spanish lady, she survived and made a good recovery. Ten months later in 2011, at the age of seventy-seven, she got a manager's job in a shop. But soon her immune system deteriorated and the cancer spread.

By this stage, I had done a lot of research into health and the human body and I wanted to know what had happened to Mum, and more importantly, how I could help her.

She came to stay with me in Australia for five weeks and I encouraged her to change her diet, rest and sleep well, and walk every day for thirty to forty-five minutes. She initially panicked but in time came to enjoy it. After a couple of weeks of this new routine, there was another problem – she was running out of her blood-pressure medication.

She said to me, 'What am I going to do after it's finished? I'll get sick. I might have a heart attack.' After five days without medication, I took her to a doctor to reassure her and check if everything was okay.

It turned out she had lost five kilos in three weeks. Her blood pressure was normal. Her mood had improved. She was so happy, and at the same time, she couldn't believe it. Tragically, as soon as she returned to Brazil, she got back into her old routines and everything fell apart again. Her health deteriorated, the cancer took hold, and the doctor told us there was nothing more he could do. She tried to go back to the routine we'd established in Australia, but it was too late. We could only hold on to her for another six months.

My beautiful mum passed away in January 2013. I couldn't keep her alive and I was understandably devastated. But it was another defining moment for me – I became even more passionate about health, performance and longevity. And I became even more determined to help people become who they wanted to be – to wake up to the life they were truly meant to live.

THE BACTERIA

It's crazy to think that what happens on a microscopic level can have a massive impact on our health and wellbeing. Take something like simple bacteria, for example.

In 2015, after a trip to Japan, I came home drained of energy. I told myself, I'm just tired from the trip – a lot of walking, flights, sleeping poorly, long hours coaching. I'll be okay in a few days. I'll get better. I just need a good rest, plenty of water and organic food. A few days later I started to get back into my training routine – weights, movement, surfing and cardio. But after my first session, my body became very sore – more than usual – and I felt even more fatigued. The next day when I got up I couldn't eat. I didn't feel like going for a surf or training. I was dragging myself around, which is very strange for me. I decided to push myself to train again, but my energy levels plummeted further, and it took me several days to recover from even my most basic routine. My brain was foggy, but I'm stubborn, so I kept pushing.

After three weeks in the same lethargic state, I was at a loss. I began to think about what was missing in my life. Diet, rest, supplements, water, the right food . . . it all checked out. But obviously something wasn't right. So I went to the doctor for some blood tests, and we found that my immune system was compromised, my neutrophils (a type of white blood cell) were very low, and I was depleted of protein. The doctor didn't have an answer; he told me it could be cancer, but he couldn't confirm it or say which type it was.

He referred me to a haematologist who specialised in cancer. Before the haematologist said anything he sent me for comprehensive blood and breathing tests, checking for almost every imaginable disease (HIV, hepatitis A, B, C . . .) as well as all types of harmful bacteria. Two weeks later I got the results. Needless to say, I was scared, and I was praying continually. The doctor went through everything. To my relief, my blood was okay – I didn't have cancer – but they'd found a lot of a type of bacteria in my gut called 'heliobacteria'. And too many isn't good. You usually contract heliobacteria from contaminated food, water or utensils. It's more common in countries or communities that lack clean water or a good sewerage system. You can also pick it up through contact with the saliva or other body fluids of infected people. My partner had to do some tests to check if she had heliobacteria too. We found that she did, but not in the same number I had, or to the same degree.

The heliobacteria were contributing to my fatigue by significantly altering my ability to extract nutrients from food. If I didn't treat the bacteria, they could cause gastritis – an inflammation of the stomach. Gastritis can also become peptic ulcer disease or stomach cancer if left unchecked. Luckily for me I'd found the heliobacteria in time.

I started researching if I could heal myself in a natural way, and visited three different naturopaths. I took away valuable information from each, but all three said the same thing: I couldn't escape taking antibiotics, but I could combine a specific diet, supplements and antibiotics to try to lower the amount of heliobacteria in my system. The interesting thing was that my partner had to take the same antibiotics as me: two different types – and heavy ones – for two weeks.

We did as we were instructed and after two weeks my partner got better, but I stayed the same. Nothing had changed! The antibiotics hadn't killed off the heliobacteria, so I had to take another two different courses of antibiotics, even stronger than the first two. I was still weak and tired, the bacteria having damaged my gut. Everything was going downhill, even my hormone levels. The healing process was long, and it took me seven months to get back to normal. The second lot of antibiotics had worked, but I also had to restore everything from the inside out – my levels of vitamins, minerals, hormones – using the right supplements, a strict diet, meditation, gentle exercise and a sauna to aid recovery. What an experience! I learned so much from my research into bacteria and parasites, the gut lining, hormones, depression, blood performance and the liver. Most importantly, I learned how not having the right balance in the body's chemistry can ruin your life, even when you think you're living as healthily as possible.

MY METHODOLOGY

We all experience good and bad cycles throughout the year. And these cycles repeat themselves across our entire life. They come and go with such regularity that many people don't recognise or even *know* what this circle of life – this journey – we're all on is like. We just think, *I'm just getting old – it's normal! I have to work harder and make money – there's no time for myself! I'm married with two kids and don't need anything! I'm forty and I deserve to have my big belly! I'm fifty and have been successful – I can drink every day! I've earned it!*

Over the years, I've heard every imaginable excuse from my clients for why they can't change their health. Instead of living a balanced life incorporating a good diet, exercise, breathwork and meditation, it's much easier to take your foot off the accelerator. But we must never stop learning. And we must never stop improving. I've found that the best master is the one who knows everything, but doesn't know anything; the one who still keeps learning from life and sharing those experiences with others.

For all these reasons, I decided to start The Art of Longevity workshops to share what I've learned and open people's eyes to their potential. I complemented the workshops with insights my good friend, two-time world surfing champion, Tom Carroll, has shared with me, along with the benefits that regular meditation and breathwork can have on the mind and body. It's been a pleasure and privilege to have Tom on this journey.

For those who don't know me, my name is Rodrigo Berthona Perez, but everyone calls me Rod here in Australia. I migrated from Brazil in 2001 after I finished my university degree in Exercise Science. I was chasing a dream of living close to the beach, continuing to improve my surfing, and coaching people from the amateur level all the way up the ranks to the top pros. My life has been all about setting goals to get to where I want to be – as an athlete, as a partner and father, and as someone who wants to keep pushing my limits until I no longer can. I still have a lot more to achieve, but having dreams is how I maintain my focus on the present, stick to my routines and continue to finetune my methods.

Over the years, I've helped and trained countless surfers, from pro-tour champions, to groms, to regular weekend warriors. I've also worked with runners, hikers, cyclists and martial artists – basically anyone who is committed to improving themselves, no matter their discipline or interests. The Holistica Movement Method I've developed has helped them all to enhance the way they move. They've become more aware of their body, they've improved their nutrition and their training, and ultimately, they've become more *durable* and better able to live a long and healthy life.

The Art of Longevity is a wake-up call, a book filled with practical, easy-to-understand principles to apply across your life – what you eat, your daily habits, your exercise goals, your meditation and breathing practices, how you recover, your lifestyle choices and much, much more.

A comprehensive list of references is available on my website, www.holisticph.com.

1.
THE IMPORTANCE OF ESTABLISHING A ROUTINE

'Routine' – what a word!

But don't be alarmed. A routine simply means certain steps or activities you follow every day. A routine can be the mechanical performance of specific acts – say, household chores – but a routine is also the basis for those more meaningful and dynamic life practices from which your happiness, health and vitality spring. A routine is a great way of navigating the cluttered forest of your mind and all the barriers your body places in front of you.

Maintaining healthy routines will improve your sleep, help you recover from injury, reduce your risk of anxiety and depression, stimulate dopamine (the 'happy chemical' our brain produces naturally), boost your memory, and have a positive effect on your mental health. Indeed, good routines have been proven again and again to have far-reaching psychological benefits.

As you've probably already guessed, routines, in essence, are centred in the mind, and practising good routines boosts our 'cognitive function': that is, our capacity to learn, think, reason, remember the past, solve problems and make decisions. With good routines, your brain starts processing things faster; your attention span becomes longer; and your endurance and athletic performance become more robust.

Our cognitive function comprises six key areas:

Complex attention: this is the ability to focus on multiple things at once. We use this faculty when we choose what to pay attention to – and what to ignore. It allows us to sustain attention and process our thoughts with speed and efficiency.

Executive function: this is the ability to prioritise, make decisions, respond to our environment and switch between tasks. Executive function allows us to plan our life, make decisions, have a working memory, respond to feedback, and inhibit certain thoughts and actions while choosing others. It also allows us to be flexible in our thinking.

Learning and memory: this is the ability to recall and record information, such as facts or events, and retrieve that information readily when needed. A healthy brain is able to digest and analyse what people are saying, whether it's during an important business meeting or in casual conversation. It allows us to recall freely and on cue, and recall memories from different points in our life.

Language: this is simply the ability to communicate, whether through writing or speaking. For me, language has always been a bit of a challenge! Born in Brazil, where the main language is Portuguese, with a Spanish-speaking mother teaching me in her native tongue, I moved to Australia to learn English, build my life and chase my dreams. I had to pretty much start from scratch, but I've embraced the challenge and continue to improve every day. Language allows us to navigate the world by naming and identifying things; while our vocabulary allows us to express ourselves and engage in meaningful relationships with others.

Perception/motor control (one of the most important cognitive functions for our physical development): this is the ability to coordinate the contraction of our muscles with the impulses sent from the motor cortex (in the brain) to its motor units (our body and limbs). It's the process of initiating and directing purposeful action.

1. The motor cortex is located in a part of the brain known as the cerebral cortex, which is involved in the planning, control and execution of voluntary movements. The cerebral cortex says to us, 'Let's take some action!' And hopefully our body responds accordingly. That action might be learning a new sport or improving your performance and graduating to the next level in some other physical activity. It might be riding a bike, walking every day, surfing for the first time, running your favourite trail, jumping for a rebound in basketball, rolling in Brazilian jiu-jitsu or lifting weights. Whatever the action, our motor learning and motor control are the results of sophisticated mechanisms at work inside

of us. Maintaining motor control also plays a big role in rehabilitation when we're injured or suffering from other health setbacks.

2. Messages from our brain's motor cortex enable us to move through a complex network of 'neural pathways'. Lifting a weight might seem simple, but in order to lift that weight, there's a huge amount of neural activity going on. Reinforcing our neural pathways and moving efficiently and purposefully is essential when it comes to improving our long-term performance and overall wellbeing.

3. The more you move and the more your body learns new things, the more you develop new neural pathways. Challenging experiences will push you to solve problems. Your mind will grow along with your body. Knowing more about the connections between motor control and motor learning will help you understand the importance of routine. We'll investigate this in greater depth later in the book.

Social cognition: this is the ability to process, remember and use the information from social interactions and conversations to explain and predict our own and others' behaviour. This is the part of our mind that controls our desires to stop us acting on impulse alone. It allows us to express empathy, recognise social cues, read facial expressions and motivate ourselves.

1. Social cognition governs how our brain and body act when we're having a conversation with friends, parents, children,

colleagues, baristas, bosses – anyone we come into contact with during the course of our day. We communicate these messages through our expressions and reactions. We assign mental states to other people, and use this to explain and predict their actions.

2. However, sometimes these social cues can be missed or misinterpreted because we're tired, in a bad mood, not eating properly, are dehydrated, or maybe because we're suffering deeper psychological conditions like depression or anxiety. Sometimes people withdraw because they have 'low energy' or can't think of anything to share with others. This lack of meaningful connection can make them feel like their life is boring, or they don't want to be a burden on others, or they're better off alone.

Understanding these basic cognitive functions will help you appreciate how routines improve your mental health and wellbeing. Our brain has to be updated all the time with new software to keep the machinery running, and continually upgrading our minds with *new* information keeps us enthused.

Let me explain what good cognitive health looks like.

The World Health Organization defines 'health' as a positive state of physical, mental and social wellbeing. They focus on the positive aspects of routine and the proactive prevention of injury and disease through physical exercise, mental challenges and stimulation, nutrition and social skills training. If we establish healthy routines – the earlier the better – we improve our own health and wellbeing and pass those values on to the next generation. The ultimate aim is to create a happiness and lust for life that will stick around for the long term.

COGNITIVE HEALTH: STAYING SHARP

We define 'wellbeing' in many different ways: living longer, having good physical health, eating well, maintaining a positive mental outlook and a good memory, being intellectually engaged and having an active social life.

Brain health is a starting point, but the next step is connecting those cognitive functions mentioned above with our *entire* being. The mind and the body are tightly connected; they have to work harmoniously together for us to function as a whole. A fit body isn't always an indication of an optimally functioning person. We need to address all the pieces and ensure they're all working well together.

Establishing positive routines does this. In order to stay sharp, we need routines in four key areas. First, we need to exercise. Second, we need to eat well. Third, we need to do simple meditation and breathwork (even five minutes a day will have a big effect). And fourth, we need to be active in society and our community – have the right people around us and engage with the outside world while doing the activities we love. Life is constantly changing: it's accepting and adapting to those changes that defines who we are. Good routines bring all four of these elements together and this is the cornerstone to longevity.

Here's my three-part formula:

Routine provides discipline

A healthy daily routine that incorporates exercise/movement, nutrition, meditation and social connection can have a powerful impact on physical and mental wellbeing. This makes us more likely to stick to the routine. Over time you develop a code of behaviour; you become committed to the routine that keeps your brain and body sharp.

Discipline gives focus

Once you've committed to your routine, you have a clearer understanding of the world and your place in it. You can define and know your dreams and goals; you can *feel* what your best life consists of and what it should look like. That clear vision becomes your central point of focus and helps you stay sharp.

Focus gives determination

Focus improves your determination. It is very important to persist in the face of life's difficulties, to recognise the pitfalls and make any changes necessary to stay true to your vision. Focus makes us fearless; we forge ahead with faith that our goals will be achieved and we can overcome any obstacles along the way.

Most of us fail in our goals because our determination is weak at the start. We lose focus and discipline, and our routines crumble under the stress. In the chapters to come, I'll give you simple, practical ways to apply my formula to your own life, without being dogmatic or imposing onerous restrictions. You can still live the life you want, but with that extra boost – a life 'amplified'.

But before we do that, there are some basic questions we need to ask ourselves. What changes would you like to see in your life? Improvement in sports performance? Improved mobility and flexibility? Less stress? Better moods? Is there an injury you want to overcome? Do you want to sort out your nutrition? Do you want to just be happier?

It takes commitment and hard work to improve your life; it's not easy and there's much to do if you don't want your dreams to pass you by.

In Chapter 10 I examine the samurai way – a commitment to a daily practice, changing and improving your life through discipline. The samurai employed a gruelling training regime so that they could remain calm, composed and prepared for battle. It was a life of extreme focus and material privation. Although the samurai's traditional training and way of life are too radical for today's world, their state of complete physical, mental and social wellbeing provides us with valuable tips for our own path to optimal health and wellbeing.

'If you calm your own mind and discern the inner minds of others, that may be called the foremost art of war.' SAMURAI SUZUKI SHOSAN (1579–1655)

'When you manage to overcome your own mind, you overcome myriad concerns, rise above all things, and are free. When you are overcome by your own mind, you are burdened by myriad concerns, subordinate to things,

unable to rise above. Mind your mind; guard
it resolutely. Since it is the mind that confuses
the mind, don't let your mind give in to your
mind.' SAMURAI KAIBARA EKKEN (1630–1714)

Thankfully, most of us aren't headed off to war, but we all face our own trials and tribulations – whether that's at work, at home, or on the sporting field. We get up every day and are confronted with new challenges; we get stressed with the load we have to carry; we have to negotiate with all kinds of people; we have to look after family members – and through it all, we still have to be in charge of our own health and put ourselves first every now and then. Developing and maintaining a calm interior is vital, and matching it with a strong sense of purpose, discipline and commitment is the foundation of healthy daily routines.

It's easy to stumble and give up – neglecting our diet, skipping the gym or rehab – especially when we're taken out of our routine by work, travel or other responsibilities. Success in life is a process of selection and elimination, of choosing between what is worthy of your time and attention, and what is holding you back.

We don't have to tackle all these things at once. There's no rush. We can discover the path to longevity gradually, if we stick with acquiring a small amount of information every day, creating new neural pathways and habits. So be patient; the results will come. Have faith and courage in yourself and don't give up at the first hurdle.

A good routine, ironically, will make us more creative and more imaginative in our approach to our health; and the benefits will be even greater. Don't be discouraged. Don't give up on yourself and the process of transforming your life. Do your best in all that you do – it might feel like you're just taking baby steps, but they're steps in the right direction.

Unless we aim to live an inspired life, we won't be able to enjoy the beautiful world in the way that we find most rewarding – the next surf, hike, trail run, yoga session . . . whatever keeps you motivated.

The first step in re-educating your body is to assess your current performance. By this I mean understanding your current state of health, accepting where you are, admitting to some of the less helpful habits you might have fallen into and examining what needs to change. Ask yourself: how long have I been in my current state – months, years, decades? Bad habits are built and reinforced over a long period of time. Declines in our health can be imperceptible, so, similarly, improvements won't happen overnight. Optimal health is not some magic pill you can take. Breaking down bad habits and building new ones takes time, persistence – and routines. Are you ready? The planning and hard work starts now!

2.
CREATING A NEW ROUTINE THAT WORKS FOR YOU

As we discussed in the previous chapter, the way you conduct your day – consciously and unconsciously – fundamentally affects your overall wellbeing. In fact, what you do *every day* matters far more than what you do *occasionally*. So, creating a brand-new routine is the first step if you want to transform your life and become healthier, happier and more energetic.

Of course, creating that brand-new routine won't be easy – but it *will* be rewarding. Many of us struggle to stick with the routines we create, even if they're tailored to our unique needs and preferences. Fortunately, a new routine doesn't have to be complicated or overwhelming. By simply maintaining positive habits and focusing on your long-term gains, you'll be well on your way.

One important factor to consider when creating a new routine is our environment. Ensuring our surroundings are conducive to productivity and positivity is essential. By 'environment' I'm talking about our workspace, home, or any other place we regularly frequent. Keeping these spaces well organised and clutter-free will help us stay focused and motivated throughout the day.

HOW CONSISTENCY CAN BENEFIT YOUR HEALTH AND LONGEVITY

In today's fast-paced world, it is easy to get caught up in the hustle and bustle. With endless tasks to complete, deadlines to meet and responsibilities to take care of, it can be challenging to find time for the things that matter most, like looking after our health and wellbeing. That's why it's vital to have a manageable routine you can control.

The benefits of a good routine include:

Better sleep quality: our bodies thrive on consistency, and by waking up and going to bed at the same time every day, we can help regulate our 'circadian rhythms' – those physical, mental and behavioural processes that run according to the body's internal clock at different times of the day. Our circadian rhythms are especially responsive to light and dark. Getting those rhythms into alignment leads to improved sleep quality and quantity, which will have a profound impact on our overall health and wellbeing.

Reduced stress levels: you just can't avoid it, stress is a constant in our lives, but implementing a routine can help reduce its negative effects. When we have a routine, we have a better idea of what we can expect from the day, allowing us to control those things we can control so we can better address any negative feelings that may arise.

Increased productivity: having a routine can also increase productivity. When we have a set schedule, we are more likely to stay focused and motivated. By breaking down our day into small, manageable tasks, we avoid feeling overwhelmed. We are more aware of what we've accomplished and are encouraged to continue along the path of having routines. We become more efficient at work and at home.

Improved physical health: by sticking to a consistent exercise routine and a healthy diet, we reduce our risk of chronic illnesses such as heart disease, obesity and diabetes. Additionally, regular exercise can improve our cardiovascular health, boost our immune system and do wonders for our mental health.

It's important to identify your goals and understand your current routine in order to create your new one. What does your ideal life look like? What activities do you want to do long into the future? What's held you back in the past? What happened in the moments when you put off long-term health for temporary satisfaction?

To ensure your new routine works and lasts well into the future, start small by creating achievable goals. From there, make sure you reward yourself for completing your goals. Creating a new routine can seem daunting at first, but improving our longevity and overall health is worth the effort.

Remember, success takes time, so be patient and try to enjoy the journey!

One of the keys to creating a successful routine is to keep a schedule. You need to determine the best time of day for your new healthy habits and then schedule them into your calendar. Be practical and realistic. Set reminders on your phone or computer to ensure you remember. A schedule will help you stay on track and make your new routine a regular part of your life.

In this chapter, I will share an epic morning routine – starting with wake-up thoughts, moving on to simple movements and breathing and meditation exercises – as well as a night routine which will help you relax and improve your recovery and sleep hygiene. The morning routine takes about 30 minutes, while the night routine only takes 10 to 15 minutes.

Remember:

Start small: a common mistake people make when establishing a new routine is trying to do too much at once. So start with baby steps. Starting with small, achievable goals will keep you calm and energised. Choose one habit you want to develop or change, and focus on it until it becomes second nature. Move on to the next challenge as soon as you successfully integrate that habit into your life.

Be consistent: consistency is key when developing healthy habits, and 'consistency' is one word you will hear repeatedly throughout the book. We are committing to a specific plan and a greater vision. This might mean setting aside a specific time for exercise, keeping healthy snacks on hand when you have cravings, or setting up a regular sleep schedule to align yourself with your circadian rhythms. If you want to dial into your circadian rhythms, say goodbye to your alarm for a few days or a week. I know it will be hard – life calls! – but a small sacrifice will allow you to observe your body's natural wake time. Another way you can reset your body is by swapping your bedside lamp for the sun's natural patterns. Open your blinds and let the light and sounds from the outside world in. It's not for everyone, but going camping for a weekend is a great way to do this!

Get support: making changes to our routine – especially if you are used to doing things a certain way, or if you have heavy work or family demands – can be hard. To increase your chances of success, find someone who can offer support – friends, a coach, or a family member. Ask this person to check in with you, encourage you, and help you stay on track with your new routine.

Celebrate your successes: acknowledge and celebrate your successes along the way, no matter how small they may seem – enjoying birdsong during a sunrise walk, staying out in the water for ten more minutes and catching one more wave, losing a couple of kilos after a long plateau. Positive reinforcement can help motivate you to continue making progress and stick with your new routine. Celebrate the little wins with a healthy treat, a relaxing activity, or simply a few words of self-affirmation.

Be flexible: remember that creating a new routine is not a 'one-size-fits-all' process. Be aware that you may need to adjust your routine as you go based on what works and what doesn't. Be open to making changes, and don't beat yourself up if things don't go as planned. The most important thing is to keep moving forward and staying committed to your goal.

People often ask me what's the best exercise to fix their shoulder, their neck, their knee, or to improve their core strength. It's human nature to seek out a magic pill or a quick fix, but it doesn't work like that. In order to attain optimal health, there are many important variables that we need to address: mobility, stability and core strength, lifestyle, nutrition and gut health, hydration and sleep. Basically, we need to take a 'holistic' approach.

No one knows your body better than you, but a couple of exercises or stretches won't give you the lasting change you're after. It will take an entirely new routine to improve your health and reduce the barriers that limit your longevity.

The first step is restoring your movement and range of motion. The simple, safe routines I'll show you will free you from restriction, and increase your physical capacity and flow. We'll cover:

A morning and night routine: you'll need to practise the morning routine at least five days out of seven, with two rest days. Given the pace of modern life, practise the night routine at least four days a week (preferably more), depending on your commitments.

For the **morning routine** we will cover neuromuscular exercises, variation of body mobility, core activation, spine alignment and decompression, stretches, stability and breathwork to increase blood flow and allow your body to be awake to meet the demands of the day.

For the **night routine** we will use a foam roller to apply gentle soft-tissue work to your body and simple breathwork to get you to sleep.

THE MORNING ROUTINE RITUAL

A good morning routine is essential for both overall health and longevity. Research has shown that people who maintain healthy and consistent habits live longer and healthier lives. You may have heard the saying, 'Early to bed and early to rise makes a person healthy, wealthy and wise.' While it's debatable whether waking up early can increase your bank balance or give you profound insights, establishing a good morning routine will help us achieve our main goal: overall health and longevity.

Daily routines might include waking up early, drinking plenty of water before our day gets busy, stretching or light exercise, meditating, writing in a journal to collect our thoughts and stimulate our imagination, and eating a healthy breakfast. Doing these activities every day will improve mental and physical health and increase energy levels throughout the day. We're more productive when we start our day early. Having an early morning routine will make it easier to focus on completing tasks and staying organised, as well as reducing stress levels and improving our overall mood.

To get started on your morning routine ritual, it's essential to first figure out what works best for you – not everyone gets their stoke from a sunrise surf, or going to a bootcamp or on a trail run! Make sure that each activity is tailored to meet your specific needs.

For example, if you find meditation helpful, make sure to find the right type of meditation. Yoga is one of the world's oldest methodologies, combining practice and bodily discipline. Two important concepts that we can take from yoga are *Abhyasa* and *Vairagya*.

Abhyasa is one of the foundational words in Hinduism and yoga. It comes from the Sanskrit word meaning 'practice'. By giving ourselves over to a daily discipline of stretching and movement, our minds will be more tranquil, and we'll achieve harmony within ourselves.

There are three essentials to *Abhyasa* yoga: practising without interruption, practising for longer periods of time, and remaining committed to the practice even when the going gets tough. The results are cumulative; the more you practise, the more addictive it becomes, and the greater the results.

The other important yoga concept is *Vairagya*, a Sanskrit word meaning 'detachment' or 'dispassion'. When we go through our morning routine, detachment allows us to release from the demands of the world and those things that vie for our attention, getting us caught up in the 'rat race' for success, approval and comfort.

From *Abhyasa*, we take the importance of effort, willpower

and regular practice. From *Vairagya*, we allow ourselves to detach from the world, accept who we are and forget the demands on our life (even if only temporarily).

Introducing these two concepts into our daily practice will give us that balance between effort and ease, and between discipline and freedom. Yoga has evolved over 5000 years and it's one of my favourite philosophies to build health and balance in my life.

If you practise your routine just once a week, once a fortnight, or once a month, it's going to be impossible to improve your health and wellbeing. Do you consider personal hygiene to be a discipline? Do you have a shower once a week, once a fortnight, or once a month? Probably not. Most of us shower daily. It helps us feel refreshed. The morning routine will come to mean the same thing for you: an essential way to refresh your body and mind and feel energised for the day.

You don't need to reach superhuman standards in your routines. We're just looking at getting back to a baseline level of body functionality and good mental health. In the short term, the goal is always to try to move and reclaim an idea of 'normal' functioning. Listen to your body and where it feels sluggish, or where you feel tight, restricted or compromised. Trust the process. Don't rush it; everything will happen at the right time with practice and persistence.

If you experience big increases in your range of motion and energy levels in just a week, it doesn't mean you are a new person. Studies suggest that it can take up to *two years* practising a new routine to make meaningful and lasting changes in the fascia (the thin casing of connective tissue that surrounds and holds every organ, blood vessel, bone, nerve fibre and muscle in place), as well as a lasting mind–body connection. You can't just do your new routine for a couple of weeks and then quit or get distracted by your 'old' life. It must be a daily commitment sustained over a long period of time.

The main motivation for creating a good daily routine is to address the restrictions that come about through our daily life (work, raising children, caring for parents, etc.). Cultivating a daily routine is not just about releasing some back tightness; it's about resetting our entire self. Many people have spent so long in dysfunctional patterns and unsustainable positions that their muscles will no longer enable them to move freely. They can no longer surf, cycle, run, have a hit of tennis or go for a long bushwalk. But if we work on restoring the full function of the tissues, joints and nervous system, we will get into better shape to increase longevity, move efficiently, and apply our conditioning without being mechanically compromised.

Do you wake up in the morning feeling tight, maybe with lower back pain or a foggy brain? These feelings can slow down your day, and can make basic tasks more difficult and more stressful to complete. Maybe the day before you didn't drink enough water, or you had a high-stress meeting or presentation. Maybe you had an unhealthy dinner at the pub or a few too many drinks at a social function. These factors can result in high cortisol levels (a steroid hormone that your body releases when you're stressed), poor sleep and that sluggish feeling in the morning. Think about all the headaches you've woken up with as a result of poor sleep, poor hydration or a poor diet (or too much booze!). Establishing a healthy morning routine that you stick to – even after that big night out or that stressful day at work – is vital. No excuses!

Committing to a long-term routine will change many things in your body: it promotes healthy cell regrowth, improves joint pain, and sharpens motor skills and body control. You will not only recapture the missing range of motion that you took for granted when you were younger, you'll also re-educate your body about what you're capable of. From this baseline you'll be able to build towards new goals.

The routine will also trigger your 'sympathetic nervous system', which helps us respond to increased physical and psychological demands. That's the part of ourselves we tap into when we get ready to jump on a board and paddle out, go into a tricky meeting at work or take on an unexpected challenge. The aim is to be warmed up and ready to face the physical and mental challenges of the day. You definitely don't need much equipment – no expensive gym memberships are required. A yoga mat and your body weight are more than enough.

You can use an inexpensive foam roller and massage ball at night or after your training session; they work on the 'parasympathetic nervous system', the flipside of the sympathetic nervous system that allows us to wind down at the end of the day – to rest, relax the body, soothe our muscles and conserve energy for the night routine. Engaging the parasympathetic nervous system will give you the same feeling you get after a massage.

As mentioned earlier, what we do *every day* is more important than what we do *occasionally*. Take a routine like brushing your teeth. How often do you brush? You don't do it once a week. And you definitely don't do it once a month. If you don't brush your teeth morning and night (and maybe during the day), you're likely to develop gum disease and tooth decay. Your friends and workmates won't appreciate it, and your dentist's bill will go through the roof! The morning routine works in a similar way. By devoting about 30 minutes a day, at least five days out of seven, to improving our mobility, rehabbing sore muscles, correcting dysfunctional movement, improving posture, and addressing niggles that precede injury, we will become a better surfer, runner, golfer, parent and/or grandparent. Remember, the ultimate goal is to improve our longevity and long-term happiness – extending the time we have to do the things that enrich and transform our life.

Of course, your goal doesn't have to be becoming an elite athlete; it's about getting back into the baseline level of fitness needed for proper functioning, and building from there. So listen to your body, and let it flow. Don't stand in its way, and stay on the path. Keep at it until the movements feel easier and you start to see incremental results. From there we'll move on to the next level.

THE IMPORTANCE OF FOCUS WHEN IT COMES TO ROUTINE

As we age, we start to realise the importance of staying healthy and fit. Longevity becomes a priority; we want to ensure we can enjoy our lives and the time we have left to the fullest. However, staying focused on our health goals can be difficult when there are so many distractions. But the unavoidable truth is that maintaining focus is crucial for improving our longevity and overall health. Having a clear focus helps us manage our time and resources better. We can more easily identify the most important tasks and plan accordingly. Paradoxically, by focusing on the present moment through movement and mindfulness, we get closer to our ultimate, higher goals. We achieve our potential by looking within and living in the now.

Focus gives us direction in life and encourages us to live each moment with intention. When we take the time to focus on what is meaningful and worthwhile, we reap the rewards of a life lived with purpose.

Establishing a routine that incorporates focus lays the foundations for pursuing any endeavour. Without focused action, burnout – trying to do too much at once or pushing ourselves at an unrealistic pace – can quickly take hold and dampen progress, or set us back months or years. A focused approach helps pinpoint potential problems, allowing for a *proactive* rather than *reactive* strategy when tackling challenges. This plan should be continually updated with lessons learned and successes realised so that goals can be kept on track. Keep a journal or a planner and write everything down; chart your progress; then record and celebrate your achievements on paper. Reflect on your setbacks and why they might have happened. Watch as your story writes itself.

Having focus is essential for success in any venture, and a routine can help provide the structure needed to maintain that focus. Additionally, tools like visualisation and positive affirmations can boost focus. Visualising exactly what you are striving for can help to keep motivation high and give a better perspective when dealing with obstacles. Positive affirmations, such as speaking positively about yourself and your capabilities, or listening to or reading self-help or inspirational books by people established on the wellness path, can also act as a powerful motivator.

Allowing time for self-care is another way to stay focused on your goals; self-care provides a much-needed break from the business of day-to-day life. Taking a few minutes for yourself can help you recharge and allow you to pursue tasks with renewed vigour and enthusiasm. Are there activities that are wasting your time or not providing any benefit? Identifying them and taking steps to eliminate them or lessen their impact will help free up more time for you to focus on your goals. Take a step back from time to time to assess your progress and make any necessary adjustments to your routine. Doing so will help ensure that your goals are kept in sight and that you remain focused on what matters most. In summary, maintaining focus:

- Enhances concentration
- Reduces stress levels
- Increases productivity
- Improves memory and cognitive abilities
- Enables better decision-making.

DISCIPLINE GIVES YOU DIRECTION

Like it or not, discipline is an integral part of life, providing structure and direction. Regularly exercising, eating nutritious meals and getting sufficient sleep are just a few disciplines that positively affect your health and wellbeing.

We live in a world that glorifies instant gratification and spontaneity. However, the truth is that most successful people (however we define 'success') are highly disciplined in their daily habits and routines. They regularly exercise, eat well and make time for themselves. They're curious about learning and growing, they stay on track with their goals, and they recognise, record and celebrate their progress.

Learning how to manage time effectively is so vital in staying disciplined; it allows you to prioritise tasks while still leaving room for relaxation and fun. Balance is fundamental for long-term success. Establishing a routine and learning how to manage stress will help maintain physical and mental health while we work towards our goals. Additionally, making time for relaxation and reflection will reduce stress levels while allowing you to stay focused on the task at hand.

Remember to take it one step at a time – and that you have all the power within you to achieve whatever you set your mind to!

THE IMPORTANCE OF DIRECTION IN ACHIEVING YOUR GOALS

Many people strive to achieve their life goals, whether it be their careers, their fitness, their relationships, or their own personal growth. However, not everyone succeeds, no matter how much effort they put in. One of the main reasons for this is a lack of a clear *direction*. Without direction, they find themselves aimlessly wandering, their goals becoming little more than distant dreams. Let's consider your routines and how to maintain direction:

Maintain a clarity of purpose: if you want to achieve your goals, it is essential to have a clear purpose, which will only come from the focus and direction you give it. While forming this purpose and direction, do not set goals you're not passionate about. Motivation is a finite resource, so spend it pushing in the right direction.

The trajectory of your motivation is UP: when you have a clear sense of direction, you will clearly see your progress and stay motivated. Of course there will be setbacks, times when you'll feel lost, confused and uncertain. But stay on track and push through the lulls and plateaus, even when the going gets tough.

Control what you can control: having direction helps you to feel in control of your life. When you know where you're going, you make better decisions. When you lack direction, it's easy to feel at the mercy of the world and the winds of chance. A strong sense of direction gives you the power to create your destiny and determine your future.

Enhance your self-confidence: direction builds your self-confidence. Every small win builds your confidence, and you'll feel closer to your goals every day. Self-confidence makes you more likely to take the risks needed to be successful, and gives you the willpower to pursue new opportunities you might not have considered before.

Be the author of your own story: sticking to your new routine can change your beliefs about yourself. When you consistently put in the effort, staying focused and maintaining direction, you'll be well on your way to solving those problems in your body and mind that inevitably come up as we age. I'm often asked by my clients, 'I know that a routine is essential, but why can I never seem to make time for it?' Every goal you set yourself must counter the small voice inside you that is working against it. It's human nature. *Why go to all this effort when you'll probably fail? Why will this time be different? Hit the snooze button; you deserve a break. Discomfort is the real enemy.* Let's make our routines simple and achievable and silence our inner critic!

START EACH DAY WITH A WAKE-UP ROUTINE

First things first:

Start with a big smile: a big smile will help your body release serotonin – the 'happy chemical' that helps reduce stress. A burst of serotonin will sharpen your mindset for the coming day. Even if your mood upon waking is dark, smiling sets the tone, so that's the first thing to do when you wake up. You'll generate a beautiful energy even before you get out of bed, and others will notice too.

Scrape your tongue: I'm sorry to say this, but your mouth is a hotbed of bacteria, dead cells and undigested food! Scraping your tongue in the morning with anything from a commercial scraper to a toothbrush will improve your overall oral hygiene, breath odour, taste and digestion.

Hydrate: drinking one glass of water upon waking (300 to 500 ml) is much better than starting the day with a cup of coffee. Your first coffee should come one to two hours after waking up.

Hydrate more: drink a second glass of water (300 ml) with the juice from half a lemon or lime. The water can be warm.

Meditation: practise 5 to 20 minutes of breathwork and meditation (see Chapters 5 and 6).

Morning exercise routine: see pages 44–58 for a recommended exercise routine to start your day, focusing on mobility, range of motion and activating your muscles.

Read: spend 10 to 25 minutes reading something affirming or mentally stimulating. Activating your mind in this way will sharpen your attention and motivate you to solve or negotiate the problems that will inevitably arise during the day.

Just as serotonin is released in the morning to stabilise your mood, the preceding routine will release dopamine, the 'feel-good' hormone, which enhances your feelings of wellbeing and motivates you to return to those activities that boost your mood. Dopamine also helps boost your immunity. Improving the body's release of these 'natural chemical highs' will get your day off to its best start and is an essential ingredient in the art of longevity.

It's simple to do. Now, let's build on this new energy for life with some practical strategies and exercises. To learn more about the morning and night routine exercises, including instructional videos, visit my Holistic Pro Health Performance YouTube channel.

MORNING ROUTINE

I often incorporate alternate nostril breathing into my morning routine. See page 58 for a description of this technique.

NECK ROTATION:

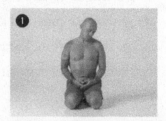

Sit in a kneeling position ❶. If you find this hard, sit cross-legged. Relax your arms, place your hands in your laps or on your thighs, and close your eyes ❷. Drop your head forward and slowly rotate it clockwise ❸ ❹. Breathe slowly through each rotation, inhaling and exhaling in a regular pattern. When you complete ten rotations, change directions.

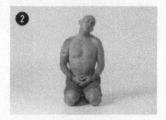

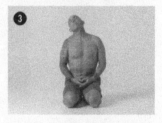

THORACIC ROTATION:

In the same kneeling or seated position, put your left hand on top of your right shoulder and your right hand on your left shoulder so your arms are crossed across your chest. Drop your head forward, chin to the chest ❶.

Squeeze yourself in a solid hug, and rotate slowly clockwise from the waist ❷. Inhale and exhale from the middle of your back (the thoracic area). Complete five rotations in each direction.

SCAPULA PUSH-UP:

From a 4-point position (the crawling position), make sure your hands and arms are in alignment with your shoulders. Keep your spine straight and long (parallel to the floor), isolating the thoracic area and engaging the scapulas (shoulder blades) ❶.

Push your scapulas towards the ceiling and then press them towards the floor (protraction and retraction), inhaling when you retract and exhaling when you protract ❷.

Remember not to bend your elbows during the movement, and keep your lower back still and stable ❸. Complete 10 reps.

SPINE WAVE:

From a 4-point position, walk your hands forward slightly, then drop your right hip towards the floor, keeping your arms straight and extending both legs behind you along the floor so your toes are now pointed away from you . Bring your arms and hands back into alignment with your shoulders to return to the upright position . Protract your shoulders, then rotate them to the right . Return to the start position , and repeat the steps towards the left. Complete 10 reps, flowing slowly through the connected movements like a wave. Exhale when you are extending and inhale when you are coming back to neutral.

KNEELING DIVE:

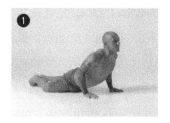

Position your body with your hips to the floor, your legs making a diamond shape behind you, back arched and arms slightly bent ❶. Slowly push your arms upwards to move into the 4-point position, with knees wide open and toes touching. (Your hands are going to move forward a little bit.) ❷ Now drive your

head forward and push your chest to the floor while keeping your arms straight. Your head will move past your hands, pushing and lifting your upper body off the floor ❸. Hold this position for a few seconds before returning to the start position. Inhale when you are moving forward and exhale when you are moving backwards.

SHOULDER OPENER:

In the 4-point position, open one arm up at the elbow and drive the other arm beneath your chest across the floor so you're reaching away from you, opening the chest as you do so . Keep this hand on the floor, opening your elbow further and expanding your chest more . Hold this position for 60–90 seconds, breathing and relaxing into the position. Repeat the action on the opposite side.

4-POINT THORACIC:

In the 4-point position, bend one arm underneath your chest and touch the opposite elbow ❶. The bent elbow should now be close to touching the floor. Inhale. As you exhale, bring the bent arm back across your body and open it out towards the ceiling, rolling across your thoracic (middle of the back) ❷. Look up and inhale before rolling back to the start position. Complete 10 reps each side ❸ ❹.

SHOULDER CAPSULE:

Lie face-down on the floor in the prone position. Tuck your left arm under your chest and extend straight out to the side 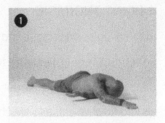. Bend your left leg at a 90-degree angle. Hold this position for 90 seconds 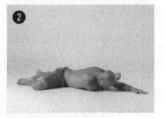. Repeat the position with the right arm and leg. Complete 10 reps.

HIP-PRONE TWIST (THE SCORPION):

Lie face-down on the floor in the prone position with arms extended perpendicular to the body. While keeping your hips as flat to the floor as you can, twist one leg across the back of your body (like a scorpion), looking in the opposite direction . Grab your foot with the opposite hand, holding onto it for 60 seconds while pressing your hips down . Make sure to inhale and exhale fully to improve the range of mobility. Repeat action with the other leg.

CALF ROLL:

Start in the 4-point position ❶, then tuck your toes, raise your knees off the floor and push them back so you are in the 'downward dog' yoga pose ❷. Now alternate moving your heels up and down in a stepping motion, trying to touch the floor with the heel each time ❸. You should feel a deep stretch through your Achilles tendon and calf muscle ❹. Inhale and exhale on each movement.

SITTING HIP ROLL:

Sit with your legs bent in front of you in an N-shape, and your arms extended behind you, palms to the floor. Roll your hips and knees from side to side. When you complete 20 reps, drop the hips as far to the right as you can, and place your right ankle on top of your left knee, applying pressure on the hip ❶. Inhale and exhale for 10 seconds then swap sides ❷.

90/90 HOLD:

Sit on the floor with the legs in the 90/90 position (as pictured) – your left leg bent in front, the right leg bent behind, hips facing forward. Place your right hand on your left ankle ❶, inhale to open the chest and slowly drop forward towards the ground ❷, walking your hand away from you so your chest and knee are aligned. Hold this position for 90 seconds ❸. Inhale and exhale to help release the muscle tension and sink deeper into the pose. Repeat on the other side.

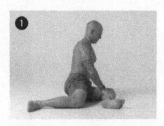

90/90 ROLL:

Sit upright on the floor in the 90/90 position and inhale ❶. Slowly turn in the direction of the leg that's bent behind you ❷, exhaling, rolling both knees up until you're in a seated position, and then fold the knees through to the opposite side ❸. Use your hands as support if needed, until you get used to the rolling movement through the hips. Then try the roll without hand support ❹. Inhale at the start position and exhale when you are rolling.

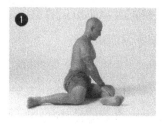

BRAZILIAN JIU-JITSU
HIP MOBILITY:

Kneel with one leg bent behind you and the other bent in front at 90 degrees . Sink your weight backwards and across your hips so your butt is closer to the floor , then step forward with your back leg . The aim is to lift your hips from the floor so your knees come down on alternating sides ❹ ❺. If you cannot get the needed lift in one motion, use a hand as support to help you through the movement. (The goal is to do it without hands.)

SITTING CROSS KICK:

From a seated position with your bent legs in front of you, inhale, engage your core and lift one leg off the floor and extend it, exhaling . Grab the foot with the opposite hand (or your calf if you can't reach), inhale and extend the leg slowly as you exhale and stretch the hamstring . Slowly release the foot and return to start position. Repeat the movement with the other leg, alternating sides for 20 reps .

TABLE SHOULDER:

Sit with your legs bent in front of you and your arms extended behind, palms to the floor. Move your hips upwards (hip extension) towards the ceiling, activating your gluteus, while keeping your elbows straight and looking up . Hold this pose for 10 seconds, then move the hips down and return to the seated position. Inhale while lowering yourself to the seated position, exhale while raising yourself up. Complete 10 reps.

STANDING DECOMPRESSION:

Stand tall (neck elongated and shoulders down), with your feet making a V-shape: big toes touching, heels apart and a slight inwards rotation of your thighs. Shift your weight back over your heels and unlock the knees. Place your thumbs at the base of your rib cage and pinkies at the top of the pelvis ❶. Inhale deeply, expanding and lifting the rib cage as much as possible as you open out your arms and splay your fingers ❷. The aim is to increase the distance between your thumbs and pinkies. As your breath deepens, your rib cage will expand in all directions. Raise your arms to chest height ❸ and bring your hands together in front of your body ❹.

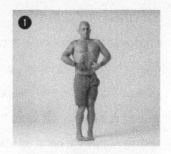

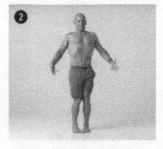

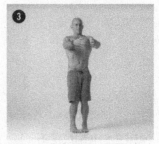

As you exhale, try to keep your upper torso in the expanded state. Continue breathing in a controlled manner – in for 3–5 seconds, out for 3–5 seconds. Repeat for 10 breaths, trying to expand your chest further each time. (Exercise credit: foundationtraining)

DEAD BUG:

Lie on your back and engage your core by pulling your navel inwards ❶. Extend your arms up from the chest towards the ceiling and raise your knees, bending your legs at a 90-degree angle as shown ❷. Moving in a slow, controlled manner, extend one leg forward while simultaneously raising the opposite arm over your head ❸. Return to the starting position before switching the movement to the opposite sides ❹.

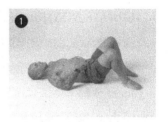

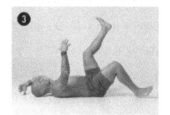

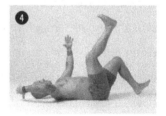

ALTERNATE NOSTRIL BREATHING:
Find a quiet place to sit, without
distractions. Bring your right hand up
to your face . Place your thumb on
your right nostril and press to close it.
With the nostril covered, close your
eyes and exhale thoroughly and slowly
through your left nostril . Once you
fully exhale, release your right nostril,
and put your ring finger on your left
nostril. Inhale deeply and slowly from
the right side. Make sure your breath is
smooth and continuous. Once you have
inhaled completely, close the right nostril
in the same manner as in the second
step and exhale through your left nostril.
When you finish the exhalation through
the left nostril, you will start to inhale
slowly through the left nostril. When it's
complete, close the left nostril in the
same manner as in the fourth step and
slowly exhale through the right nostril.
Repeat the technique for 5–10 minutes
or 10–20 reps. You can do alternate
nostril breathing for as short or long a
period as you like.

NIGHT ROUTINE

These exercises require a standard foam roller. They generally cost between $10 and $50, and are widely available at most major department stores, sporting goods stores, as well as online.

I often incorporate alternate nostril breathing into my nightly routine. See page 58 for a description of this technique.

ITB ROLL:

Lying on your side, place a foam roller perpendicular to your legs, between your knee and hip, in the middle of the thigh ❶. Slowly roll yourself up to the top of your hip (the iliac crest) ❷ and back down, applying gentle downward pressure through the movement, until you get closer to the knee. Repeat this action, inhaling as you roll up and exhaling on the way down. This will massage the ITB (iliotibial band) and the muscle running along your outer thigh (the vastus lateralis) ❸, reducing tightness. Complete 10 reps on each side.

QUAD ROLL:

Lying face-down in the push-up position, with the foam roller perpendicular to your legs between the floor and the top of your quadriceps, roll yourself down to just above the knee 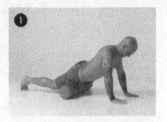, applying light pressure, and roll back up. Exhale as you roll down and inhale on the way up. You can apply additional pressure by bending one knee and shifting your weight through the hips to the opposite side 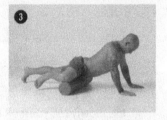. Complete 10 reps on each side.

TFL ROLL:

The TFL (tensor fasciae latae) is a small

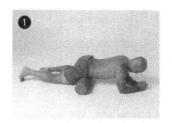

muscle at the top of the hip, just above the ITB. This is the muscle that often gets tight from sitting at a desk for long periods of time. Lying face-down in the push-up position, place the foam roller perpendicular and below your torso at the top of your hips, and lean slightly to one side ❶. Roll up and down in small movements, inhaling on the up, exhaling on the down. The TFL, being a small area, doesn't require a lot of pressure to be effective. Complete 10 reps on each side.

GLUTE ROLL:

Sit on top of the foam roller on one butt

cheek, with your left foot on top of your right knee, supporting yourself with one or two hands on the floor behind you ❶. Roll forward and backwards a few

centimetres in each direction to initiate the release of tension. The gluteus are tough muscles, so you can opt to apply extra pressure by sitting down firmly on the foam roller ❷. (If you find this painful, reduce the pressure and move more slowly.) Don't forget to breathe. Complete 10 reps on each side.

THORACIC ROLL:

Lying on your back, with your legs bent at 45 degrees, place the foam roller below you, perpendicular to your upper-middle back (the top of your thoracic area). Lock your fingers behind your head for support ❶. Inhale, engage your core and crunch your body forward ❷ and, with your feet controlling the movements, gently roll down your back as you exhale, until the foam roller reaches the bottom of the thoracic area, just below the middle of the spine ❸. Continue this breathing pattern as you roll up and down along this area. Complete 10 reps.

LOWER BACK ROLL (WITH TWIST):

Lying on your back, lift your hips and place the foam roller below you, perpendicular to your lower back area . Stay in this position without moving for 2 minutes, inhaling and exhaling slowly, allowing the foam roller to take the pressure off your lower back. Next, roll slowly down to your tailbone (the triangular sacrum below the lumbar). Alternate bringing one leg up at a time in a crosswise motion, twisting at the hip, and pulling the knee across the body with the opposite hand . (The other hand can hold the end of the foam roller for support.) Look in the direction of the support hand, deepening the twist in the spine as you exhale . Complete 10 reps on each side.

PECS:

Lie down with the foam roller to your left parallel with your body. Extend your left arm over the foam roller at chest height. Turn your head to the right and, at the same time, bend your right leg to a 90-degree angle. Place your right hand on the floor and raise your elbow, putting pressure on the left side of your chest ❶. Slightly push your right arm up and down in small movements to apply a myofascial release in the muscles. Stay there for 3–5 minutes then change sides.

SPINE BREATHING:

Lie on your back, knees bent with the foam roller running horizontally from your tailbone to the back of your head ❶. Tilt your pelvis so your spine is flat and connected to the length of the foam roller. Relax your arms on the floor, close your eyes, and inhale and exhale through the nose. Stay in this position for 5–20 minutes – and then your nightly routine is done! You are now ready for a restorative sleep.

3.

MOVE WELL, MOVE STRONGER AND MOVE FOR LIFE!

Now that we've established the framework for some basic wellbeing routines, let's get technical and talk about 'functional movement' and getting stronger – and how they relate to longevity.

Thanks to a few health issues as a kid, I started my fitness training and investigations into health at a pretty young age. Swimming really improved my lung capacity. Looking back, it probably saved me.

I learned early on – the hard way – that movement is an absolutely essential part of life. Movement allows us to carry out our everyday activities, whether we're running, lifting weights, going to the shops or simply walking the dog. As we age, our movement patterns change. Most of us experience muscle and joint pain, as well as increasingly limited mobility. We might get down on ourselves, saying things like, 'I'm not the person I used to be!' But this doesn't have to be the case. With the right mindset and the right approach, we can restore our movement and our strength and get back in the game.

Being physically active has countless health benefits, both physical and mental. But unfortunately, as we get older, people tend to do the opposite: they slow down and *reduce* their physical activity. This is understandable: we have less time, more pressing commitments from work and family, an aversion to risk; or maybe we've moved away from a specific community of physically active friends. While taking the 'path of least resistance' might seem like an easy option, it has disastrous effects on our health and wellbeing. So it's essential to reignite your motivation and make a conscious effort to stay active and keep moving, particularly as you age.

There are three key elements to living a life of movement that we'll cover in this chapter:

Moving well means moving safely and efficiently without risking injury. To move well, you must pay attention to your form and technique, especially when doing gym exercises like lifting weights, squats, deadlifts, etc. Whatever exercise you do, it's essential to start with a warm-up session to loosen your muscles and prepare your body for physical activity. Once you start feeling comfortable with your basic movements, you can gradually increase the intensity of your workout routine. Remember that moving well and re-establishing your range of motion must include recovery – properly resting between workouts and stretching. (I go into helpful methods of recovery in Chapter 8.)

Moving with strength is another crucial aspect of maintaining an active life. To increase your strength, you must gradually increase the *resistance* of your exercises. Doing so will help build and maintain muscle mass, improving your overall strength and reducing the risk of falls and other injuries. Strength training exercises like lifting weights are great ways to increase strength, but so are classic exercises that involve your own body weight, like push-ups, pull-ups and planks. As a bonus, strength training also increases bone density and reduces the incidence of osteoporosis in older adults.

Moving for life is a practice that incorporates physical activity into your daily routine. The aim is it then becomes a lifelong habit. It's not about doing strenuous exercises every single day, but rather being *active* for at least 30 minutes a day, whether you're walking, cycling, swimming, dancing or gardening. You could take up a new sport or activity, like tennis or golf, or a new hobby, like bushwalking or birdwatching. The key is to keep moving *regularly* and *consistently*.

Remember that physical activity doesn't just benefit our bodies; it also has a positive impact on our minds. Regular exercise helps reduce anxiety and depression, improves mood and cognitive function, and reduces stress levels. Being active can also improve your sleep patterns (your circadian rhythms), which will help you feel more refreshed and energised throughout the day. Your body will love the reward of a sound sleep after a session in the surf or a trail run.

Moving well, moving stronger and moving for life all contribute to a healthier and happier life. If you're new to exercise, start small and gradually increase the intensity of your movement. It will take time to see results, but as we discussed in the previous chapter, *consistency* is key. Doing something every day is more important than doing something occasionally. And of course, before starting any exercise program, talk to your physician, especially if you have underlying health conditions.

It's a boom time in the fitness industry, with more and more people looking to improve their health, lose weight, and get to the gym. Many try to go hard every day. They push themselves to lose a set amount of weight in a short time, stack on muscle quickly and get stronger by finding short-cuts. This sort of approach is just not sustainable. And it doesn't help when there is a legion of influencers wanting to show you the quick way to the new you, or products promising to help you along your journey with a magic pill or tonic. It can all be very confusing. Ignore it. Sticking to the basics is the best way to achieve longevity.

Most people struggle to understand how they can improve or change their lifestyles, or how to say no to those things that undermine their health and life goals. But there are many more who persist and want to change their life, improve their performance and build longevity. Changing our mindset and our bodies takes time, practice and the resolve to steadily move forward over the long term. We need to be open to learning new things and accepting the process behind real change.

Here's a really simple example: forget dieting! It's far better to educate yourself on how to eat well, how to nourish your body the right way, and how to extract the benefits of eating real food as nature provides it. I always advise my clients that nutrition is just as important as exercise. Good habits are hard to establish and bad habits can be very tricky to break. But we all need to discover what is best for our bodies. This initial 're-education' period can take 9 to 18 months. So be patient. (We'll discuss food and nutrition in more detail in the next chapter.)

How does all this affect training for improved movement? The same principles are at play. Don't jump into high-intensity training straightaway just because you want to lose weight now, or increase your cardio, or carve yourself those six-pack abs you saw on Instagram or TikTok. Those instructors and models look like that because they have put in the time – their look is their livelihood, after all. And forget the magic pills and tonics. The special supplements they are spruiking won't help, and some can be downright dangerous. Some of the training methods they advocate can cause damage and issues in the long term. The best path to longevity is to build your body steadily, carefully and consistently.

It's great to have lofty goals – excelling at sports, setting a PB in a distance run, or pushing your limits with high-intensity training – but first we need to create the right structure for your body, the right physical platform on which to achieve your goals. Otherwise, you'll injure yourself. Recovering from an injury can be a long and painful road, and many people give up because of the stress and strain. So remember to start with baby steps, using techniques that work best for you in order to build a sustainable foundation.

We also shouldn't train our bodies only one way. Balance your activities between stretching, mobility exercises, strength training, endurance and cardiovascular routines, breathwork and meditation, and sport. And don't forget recovery! After 25 years of coaching all sorts of people, from those with lower back, joint, hip, shoulder and knee pain to pro athletes recovering from serious injuries; people with diabetes or struggling with their weight to everyday athletes practising all different types of sports – Brazilian jiu-jitsu, capoeira, yoga, surfing, soccer, swimming, gymnastics, golf, ultra trail runners and more – one of the most important things I've learned is to incorporate a variety of *complementary* activities to your daily routine.

A lot of coaches and physicians say aerobic fitness is the key ingredient to longevity. But studies show that managing *multiple* disciplines – high-level mobility, flexibility, muscle strength, power-to-weight ratio, and coordination – have a greater influence. And of course variety keeps life more interesting and your mind stimulated! Ultimately, your body can do more than you think, and with the right mindset and the right approach, you can reach any goal. So, let's get up, get out there and start moving.

In this chapter, I explain each training 'modality' and how to tailor one of my 12-week programs to your own specific needs, whether your goal is rehab, recreational activity, or high-performance sports and competition. The programs are designed to be simple, efficient and, best of all, they require minimal equipment!

WHAT IS MOBILITY?

Mobility is the range of motion in your joints, muscles and connective tissue. Some define it as the active control of a joint when combined with strength and flexibility. Good mobility will expand the joint workplace and contribute to long-lasting changes. You will be able to move your body into an increasing variety of positions, even some that you never knew were possible! When you have established a base level of mobility, you can train harder, recover faster and perform repetitive movements over long periods of time without putting yourself at risk of injury. You're more durable. An improved range of motion also translates to more power, whether you're paddling through big sets of waves, swinging a golf club or sprinting across sand.

One of the main movement patterns we should be able to easily perform, at all ages, is squatting. But how deep can you squat without pain? Can you maintain your posture through the motion? Are you able to pick up weights or groceries or a toddler from this position? It's a simple idea, like walking freely without exertion, but it tells us a lot about our functional mobility. We don't often think of this when we're young, but soon enough we start to notice changes in our mobility, balance, coordination and strength. Simple tasks can become much more difficult; even just picking up a box from the floor or kicking a ball with the kids.

So why do we want better mobility? Well, there are many benefits:

- Decreased risk of injuries (the priority)
- Improved performance (moving smoothly in all planes)
- Improved efficiency of motion (taking a risk without injury)
- Improved joint range of motion (having more power in motion)
- Reduced muscle tension and freedom of movement (having freedom of motion and faster recovery periods)

- Improved body flow and awareness (mindfully connecting a range of motions with efficiency).

THE IMPORTANCE OF MOBILITY

Having worked over the years with people of all different body types, different ages and different needs, I can usually see quickly where mobility problems originate. Restrictions, slow movement, poor bodily awareness, diminished perception, a lack of engagement with the central nervous system, tightness and fatigue in the different movement patterns, high recurrence rate of injury, poor posture . . . an inability to touch toes! These days, the cases of hip and knee replacements are increasing, as are cases of bulging discs resulting from our sedentary lifestyles, and back surgeries are more common.

For many of the people I've helped, the main problem was that they'd never moved freely. And they'd never cared about it because it's so much a part of modern life. They didn't notice their restrictions until these basic movements became too hard and started affecting their daily life.

From those sessions, I started to give my students soft body weight movements that focused on basic mobility but had other benefits – like treating myofascial slings (stimulating the underlying fascia, muscles and tendons that support the back and spine), sharpening proprioception (how we perceive our surroundings and move through them), and working to make connective tissues more supple. Through these targeted movement exercises, I could see improvements in posture, alignment, movement and flow, deeper squats, a decrease in lower back pain, and faster healing rates.

It's important to understand the relationship between our joints and the way they all transfer forces and loads from one to the other. There are four main joints in the body: the ankle, knee, hip and shoulder. If one joint is restricted, it can create problems for the others. For example, if you have a tight ankle, it is very hard to do a nice, deep squat. A tight ankle can give us a lot of trouble with knee stability and create knee pain. It can also restrict your range of hip motion and add to poor posture and spine misalignment. A tight hip can present problems for shoulder rotations (like throwing or swimming). It can also cause lower back pain and switch off the gluteus muscles (in your backside).

Increased mobility relieves the tensions associated with both our sedentary lifestyles and our tendency to over-exercise before we've created a solid foundation. While mobility is one of our main focuses, we must always remember to complement it with strength training. Yes, you can improve your range of motion, but you must also get stronger. The body must be mobile enough to allow the muscles to do their job properly. The mental benefits? You'll feel alive, vibrant, more open to experiences, with no pressure or tightness to fight through. You'll get up in the morning happy, with more energy and improved blood flow, having given your body a chance to properly recover and your cells the opportunity to regenerate during sleep.

This is how one of my clients related the feeling of improved mobility to me:

'Mobility training has increased my mindfulness and awareness of new movements open to me. I'm living in a new world – it's a game-changer! Before I never moved from this spot, and even if I tried, I always hesitated because I was scared that my body couldn't move in that way and I'd get hurt. It is very interesting – before I could never think or move the way that I now can. It's incredible how things can start to change in only two weeks of practice, and I have been practising every day in the early morning. My lower back pain is gone, and I can flow in both hips well – and I've even had surgery on one of them!'

THE HIP JOINT AND HIP MOBILITY

The hips are made of strong, compact bone and are the power-house of the body, allowing the lower limbs to move in three different planes while also serving as a shock absorber for the upper body. The hip joint is meant to be more stable and less mobile than the shoulder joints, but if restricted the hips can do the most damage to our overall wellbeing. A lot of blood flows through the hip area, so a tight hip can increase the risk of lower back pain, knee pain and ankle pain. These days, more and more people have hip replacements because they push too hard in life without ever having a proper range of motion in their joints. This puts a lot of pressure on the top of the joints and causes repetitive damage and torn cartilage. They get to a stage where they cannot support themselves, work through the pain or function properly.

Have you heard that, when you get older, breaking your hip dramatically shortens your life expectancy? Some reports say around 50 per cent of patients who suffer a hip fracture die within six months, and many of those who survive don't ever fully recover their functionality and previous way of life. Although this mostly affects people over 60 years of age, hip awareness should start right now, whether you're in your twenties, thirties, forties or fifties.

A Brazilian physician–researcher in exercise and sports medicine, Dr Claudio Gil Araújo, has designed a test called the 'sitting-rising exercise' to predict mortality in middle-aged and older people. Published in the *European Journal of Preventive Cardiology* in 2012, the test was the cause of widespread alarm for many people who couldn't get themselves up from the floor! It requires a basic level of muscle power, coordination, body composure, balance and flexibility. One of the test's objectives was to record the number of supports (like a hand or knee) needed and the level of balance and exertion required for these actions. While the test was targeted at 51- to 85-year-olds, it's a good wake-up call for everyone to keep up with your pliability throughout your life.

The test is simple:

- Sit on the floor cross-legged, like a Buddha, and try to rise using minimal support.
- You start the test with five points. One point will be subtracted for each support you use, like a hand, forearm,

knee or side of the leg. A point is deducted if you place one hand on your knee to help sit up or rise. Another half a point will be taken off if the motion is perceived as laboured and unsteady.

• The number of points you're left with will quickly give you an idea of the degree to which you need to improve your hip mobility.

FREE HIPS = FREE FLOW – GRAHAM'S STORY

I've been working with my 64-year-old client, Graham, for about six years. He showed up at my practice after having a type of back surgery called a microdiscectomy. This is a major procedure with the patient under general anaesthetic to relieve pressure on the spine and nervous system from a herniated disc. Graham had a history of lower back pain, and in the year before the surgery he developed a foot drop (a gait abnormality where one foot 'drops' lower than the other and you're unable to raise your toes).

During the microdiscectomy surgeons removed the damaged part of the disc in Graham's spine, where its soft centre was pushing out through the tough outer lining. When Graham visited me after surgery, he was walking normally but didn't have much feeling in his left foot. His hips had terrible mobility, and there was a lot of pressure on his sacrum – the area of the lower lumbar, at the base of the spine – and he couldn't stand up from the floor without using his hands or help. He had hardly any points left after doing the 'sitting-rising exercise'!

Graham's rehabilitation was going to be long, so we began with baby steps. Despite being a strong man, he was only capable of a small number of movements – and even those were restricted. I had to completely re-educate him on how to move properly. It was a big challenge, but he came to see me five days a week and in time we made progress.

Graham realised how bad his condition was and understood that surgery alone wasn't going to fix him. We started with small movements on the floor: trying to stand up efficiently, crawling, slowly building capacity and stability, and then moved towards strength work. We had to wake up his nervous system and give his body new stimuli in order for it to regrow in a stronger way.

Today, Graham is a machine. He can hold handstands for a minute and hang from a bar for a period of time. He can do controlled squats and deadlift 140 kilograms for two reps. He rides his bike every day and has just started learning how to surf. His ability and range of motion is impressive. While it took him four years to fully accept and work through the new movements, he saw progress every day and never gave up or stopped his routine. We worked on nutrition and mindset exercises, and he reached his target weight of 78 kilograms (2 kilograms more than when he was young) – down from his peak at 94 kilograms. In short, Graham has got his life back.

LET'S GET STABLE (STABILITY TRAINING)

Along with mobility, our joints need 'stability' work too. The joints are like the foundation of a house; if they're not stable, the body collapses. A lack of stability in one joint creates instability in others. To function better, we need to get the balance right. We cannot work on our mobility but forget about our stability. Nor can we work too much on strength and power if we don't have the right foundation. I love stability work because we can challenge our nervous system by sending signals for a wide variety of different muscles, tendons and ligaments throughout the body, some of which we won't be used to using. We need to intentionally single them out.

When I design a program for someone – whether the goal is athletic performance, elite competition, rehabilitation or just an improved overall lifestyle – stability is the second-most important part of the regime. If my athletes or clients aren't able to maintain good, stable positions, I keep them from moving on to weights or other strength exercises. We start with single-leg and single-arm exercises to activate the muscles that keep us in balance, and we work to keep the spine stable and elongated through these corrective movements. Graham's regime followed this approach, combining functional body movement, mobility, reconnecting with the body's flow, and stability. It's hard to achieve this level of fitness and it's very easy to lose, especially as you get older.

There are two types of stability, 'active' and 'passive':

Active stability is when the body's mechanics respond and move based on the signals sent by the brain. We tell our body to perform a particular movement or action, and the body responds.

Passive stability is the physical hardware of the body – the bone, cartilage and ligaments – that hold us together without us having to consciously think about it.

While there are many exercises that target stability, here are two simple ones to start with. You'll find others later in this chapter.

THE SINGLE-LEG SQUAT AND THE SINGLE-LEG STAND (WITH EYES CLOSED).

Stand in front of a full-length mirror. Lift or bend one leg up, trying to keep your balance. In the next step, start to squat on the standing leg. As you lower, use your inside-leg muscles to counter your ankle instability and weak glutes. When you are going down to a squat, you will start to shake, and your knee might wobble from side to side – this is from your muscles activating to correct the instability. It's part of the strengthening process. You don't need to squat all the way down; just squat to the limits of your range of motion and then come gently back up again.

Next, and this can be surprisingly hard, try to balance on one leg. Now close your eyes. If it's hard to maintain that position for more than a few seconds, you have another point of instability that needs to be addressed.

IS THERE A DIFFERENCE BETWEEN STRETCHING AND MOBILITY?

Our bodies are made up of many different, complex systems – all intertwined with each other – and we need these systems to work together in a holistic way. The relationship between flexibility and mobility is one such system. Flexibility is the ability of a joint or series of joints to move through a full range of motions. Stretching deliberately targets a specific muscle or tendon to improve our range of motions. And good flexibility improves our general mobility, ensuring that our joints all move in an effective range. (This range of motions will vary depending on the type of joint.)

Ideally, we want to become supple like a cat – bending, twisting, jumping and executing different movements with ease and fluidity, rather than stiffness or awkwardness.

CORE WORK – LET'S BE SUPPLE FOR LIFE

Our body's core musculature is like the nucleus in an atom – it is the centre of our energy and power. It's the essential component of any movement, and it connects the upper and lower body for better functioning.

Many people make the mistake of going to the gym with the sole aim of getting buff, building big muscles and doing as many crunches as possible to get that eye-catching six-pack. A lean body, sculpted musculature and tight abs, however, don't always translate to efficiency when we're talking about functional body movements, like surfing or yoga.

Your 'core' (or trunk) plays a dominant role in every plane of motion: 'sagittal' (the plane that divides the body down the centre from head to toe); 'frontal' (the plane that divides the body from front to back); and 'transverse' (the plane that divides the body in half from the waist). When applying any manoeuvre, the nervous system anticipates the movement and braces for support, using your core. If your core does not stabilise and support the spine, your body will start compensating by using different muscles, often ones we're not used to engaging. We then start to develop muscle imbalances and increase our risk of injury.

Sports like surfing, Brazilian jiu-jitsu and gymnastics involve a complex range of motions. The body must move along these different planes, in many directions, and draw strength from the core (activation, stability, strength and power).

Common complaints you might experience when you engage in these activities with a weak core include:

- Lower-back pain
- Poor posture
- Shortness of breath
- Poor stability and balance
- Weakness in the body (shoulder, neck, hips, etc.).

The benefits of core training include:

- A strong and supported back and spine
- Improved balance and stability
- Improved connection and flow between movements (functional movement)

- Lower risk of injury
- Correct posture.

In surfing, for example, these benefits are manifested in stronger paddle strength, stable pop-ups, powerful turns, composure while catching air and landing, compressing and decompressing through turns, and a stable stance. In Brazilian jiu-jitsu and yoga, you're able to hold static poses longer and with more stability, as well as transition better between poses and movements.

The muscles that comprise your core are:

The diaphragm: the muscle below the lungs and heart that facilitates breathing.

Transverse abdominal muscles (TVA): the deepest abdominal muscles, which wrap horizontally around our sides and back and are key to preventing back pain.

The multifidus muscle: the innermost layer of back muscle that runs along the spine and is activated when you bend or extend your back.

The rectus abdominis muscle: the 'six-pack' muscle located between the ribs and extending down to the pubic bone. It controls movement between the ribs and the pelvis.

The pelvic floor: the group of muscles and ligaments that undergird the bladder, womb and bowel.

The erector spinae: the group of muscles that supports and elongates the back and spine.

Internal and external oblique muscles: the group of muscles that runs down your sides, on either side of your rectus abdominis muscle.

I break down an ideal core program into various phases:

Phase 1: Core activation (breath)

This is the foundation of a good core workout and activates your 'inner unit' abdominal muscle, and in particular the diaphragm and TVA muscles.

Do you know how to breathe through your belly? In Chapter 5 we'll discuss diaphragmatic breathing for better core function. This breath pattern is essential for human functioning.

Phase 2: Core stability (motor control, ability to transfer force)

This is the ability to keep your core activated while controlling the body's position and movement into your extremities without compensating with spine movements or the pelvic floor. Maintaining a neutral spine during activity preserves the spine and prevents injuries, allowing you to perform at your best. I emphasise this point throughout my descriptions in the 12-Week Training Plan.

Phase 3: Core strength

A stronger core will make sport and everyday life so much easier. A strong core allows you to produce force throughout a movement. The strength of the underlining muscle of the trunk helps the body maintain an ideal posture.

Examples of simple core strength exercises include:

- Dead bug (see page 57)
- Straight-arm plank (see page 119)
- Side plank variations (see pages 123 and 157)
- Sitting cross kick (see page 55)

(You can find more examples and videos on my website and YouTube channel – Holistica Movement – or by following my Instagram @holisticprohealth.)

Phase 4: Power core (the cool phase)

The 'cool phase' is where we start loading the exercises with weight and applying force through movements similar to the activity you want to pursue.

THE KEY POINTS FOR A GOOD CORE PROGRAM

- Check your breath. See if you can breathe through your diaphragm (extending your belly).
- Keep your core activated during the movement.
- Find the proper level of exercise when you begin. Don't overdo it to the point where you're in pain or risk injury.
- Do your core exercises at the *end* of your session, so you don't tire your spine and pelvic stabiliser muscles.
- Remember that good core strength is fundamental to supporting you for any sport or workout.

CARDIOVASCULAR TRAINING

Cardiovascular training decreases your resting blood pressure and heart rate and improves and increases the oxygen supply in your blood vessels. It also strengthens your body's circulatory and respiratory systems, which are essential in building stamina and endurance. Aerobic exercises can include running, dancing, walking, cycling, boxing, swimming – anything that increases your breathing and heart rate. It doesn't have to be overly strenuous, and there are plenty of ways to make it interesting, so try to fit in at least two and a half hours of aerobic exercise a week. You could do it in one long training session (not ideal) or split it into five 30-minute sessions or two 75-minute sessions – whatever suits you best.

Cardiovascular training brings many benefits, including:

- Increased blood flow, which decreases the chance of stroke
- Improved joint health and reduced risk of developing osteoporosis and hip fractures
- Improved memory and clarity of thought
- Helps fight cognitive decline (such as Alzheimer's disease)
- Helps in the management of arthritis
- Maintains stability and preserves range of motion.

SMART CARDIO

After many years of research, observation and trialling different approaches to cardio training, I have developed a science-based, sustainable, 'smart' way to keep fit.

My smart cardio durability training is divided into two different types.

The first is Long Cardio (LC) sessions, which last 45–90 minutes. I've recommended training one hour in Zone 2 (60–70 per cent maximum exertion) once a week – twice a week at an absolute maximum. Remember: everyone's perceived level of exertion is different! This allows you to build an aerobic base, enhance your endurance, optimise your fitness and unlock performance gains. Zone 2 training greatly benefits anyone, regardless of their level of activity or goals.

Zone 2 training focuses on *moderate*-intensity training. Keeping in this zone means oxygen is the primary driver of energy production. This increases your aerobic capacity. If you are interested in optimising your endurance, improving your body composition (your percentage of fat, bone and muscle), avoiding injuries and reducing the risks of overtraining, Zone 2 should be your goal.

Examples of LC sessions include brisk walking, cycling, rowing, swimming, long-distance running and hiking – activities that you can easily adjust your exertion levels to reach 60–70 per cent of your maximum heart rate.

The second approach is Short Cardio (SC). These sessions last between 10 and 15 minutes overall and consist of 10–20-second sprints of a chosen activity and a two-minute recovery period between sets. (Don't start the next set until you've fully recovered.) The aim is to get in six to ten reps during that time period. This type of training is considered Zone 4 or 5, which represents 75–95 per cent of your maximum heart rate. I recommend including SC training at least twice a week (four times at the absolute maximum).

I've found it's best to do my SC training after a weights session. If you're going to work it into your day, make sure to warm up well, and eat carbs at least two hours before you train.

This level of exertion crosses over into anaerobic training, meaning your body starts breaking down glucose for energy *without* oxygen. It's hard to sustain this level of exertion for long periods. Training in this zone is intended to improve athletic performance, speed and power.

So, Zone 4 is for anaerobic capacity training, limiting the amount of energy your body can produce anaerobically. Zone 5 is the target zone for short-burst speed training.

Longevity is about being powerful and able to react to anything life throws at you.

Examples of SC sessions: running sprints (flat, soft-sand, uphill, stairs), air bike (I love this one), rowing machine, Tabata/HIIT training (high-intensity interval training), skipping rope, burpees, boxing/sparring over two-minute rounds.

When I was young and had my respiratory complications, cardiovascular exercises helped me gain a fuller life. As my condition improved, I was able to function better and enjoy all those activities that excited me. If you haven't already, it's time to introduce cardiovascular exercises into your life. But don't overdo it. I know a lot of people who spend 30 or more minutes a day doing casual exercise – some do 60 to 90 minutes cardio every single day! Too much cardio can increase the levels of cortisol in the body, and potentially damage your muscle tissue, joints, strength capacity and skin tone. It can even push you towards adrenal fatigue. For true longevity, everything needs to be in balance and your routine kept sustainable. (I discuss recovery further in Chapter 8.)

Coming back to my client Graham, he loves riding his bike and gets out three to five days a week for 30 to 50 minutes at a clip. Some days he pushes himself harder, while other days he maintains a steady pace with a controlled heart rate. He has a healthy balance of stress and recovery. Keen runners who jog an hour a day should diversify their exercise portfolio, adding cycling, swimming, 10 to 15 minutes of sprints or even 30 minutes of circuit training at the gym. You don't need to run long distances every single day – spread it out through the week.

As I say to all my clients, no matter what activity you choose, just getting your body moving will increase your circulation, improve your mental clarity and help you along the path to longevity. And the results compound: every cardiovascular training session will increase your oxygen supply and lung capacity, allowing you to work out harder and longer over time. Your muscles will adapt, allowing you to increase your workload. In turn, your day-to-day activities will become easier.

I used to be really hard on myself when it came to cardio training. I put too much pressure on myself, but the good thing is we can all achieve a healthy balance by introducing different types of training to get the cardio going. As the cliché goes: variety is the spice of life.

USING ENDURANCE TO ACHIEVE DURABILITY

Endurance is the ability of our body to remain active over a long period, as well as its ability to resist, withstand, recover from and have immunity to trauma, wounds or fatigue. Endurance can involve *aerobic* exercise (activities where the body uses oxygen to create energy) or *anaerobic* exercise (high-intensity activities where the body starts to burn glucose without using oxygen). Endurance is often associated with gruelling events where the body is pushed to its limits, like running a marathon, completing an ironman or ironwoman competition or triathlon, or an outdoor expedition. But there are other ways to build endurance.

Sustaining an activity over a prolonged period of time has many benefits, including:

- Reducing the risk of injury
- Healthier, stronger muscles and bones
- Maintenance of a healthy body weight
- Increased confidence, self-reliance and an overall feeling of wellness
- Improved performance and stamina in everyday activities, like climbing and descending stairs, lifting boxes, chopping wood, playing with the kids, etc.
- Better posture
- Improved sporting performance
- Less fatigue over the long term.

Most importantly, endurance is key to longevity. It helps us retain muscle strength, energy levels, motivation and autonomy as we age.

One of the simplest exercises to improve your endurance is crawling. Yes, like a baby but without touching your knees on the floor!

When I designed my clinic, I included 15-metre-long mats, where I have all my students do laps of crawling. It doesn't matter what age they are, whether they're an athlete or not – they all have to do two or three sets crawling the length of the mat. I might mix in some other body movements, but all my clients have to maintain this activity over the distance. (If we have a beginner student or client at the start of rehabilitation, we'll build up to the crawl while improving their endurance, strength and stability, but the aim is always to complete the 15-metre distance. From there, we increase the number of sets.)

It's exciting to watch people develop following the initial assessment. Over the 25 years I've been working with clients, one of the main things I've observed is the ability of the body to increase its capacity over time, allowing people to continue to do the things they love to do, which is what the art of longevity is all about. Too many people break down as they age because their bodies and minds fold when met with fatigue or discomfort. Longevity is simple to say but hard to commit to. So, keep in mind these different approaches to cardio training to improve your endurance so you can pursue your goals.

PURE STRENGTH

Strength training is another area we must practise consistently – not necessarily every single day, but we should aim to do at least two to four sessions a week. Yes, that's right, we must hit the weights (or perform weight-bearing exercises) at least twice a week! Many people spend a lot of time on circuit training and cardio, endurance and stretches, but few ever stop to slow down the body to develop the right muscle groups, correct their posture, control their movements and get stronger.

Strength training also has the knock-on effect of helping you manage your weight and increase your metabolism, so you burn calories more efficiently. It helps protect your joints by developing the right muscles surrounding them to keep your base stable and your body mechanics fluid. It also helps us maintain our bone density after we turn 50, retain muscle mass and stimulate hormone production.

You might be wondering how you'll fit strength training into your busy schedule, but by following a daily routine, training will soon become a priority that complements the rest of your life rather than distracts or pulls you away from it.

I've divided the weekly workouts on the following pages into Routines A, B and C, with cardio routines mixed in.

- Routine A relates to the topics covered in Chapter 2 – mobility, stretches and movement flow.
- Routine B targets lower bodywork, from building capacity to stability and strength.
- Routine C targets upper bodywork, from building capacity to stability and strength.
- The cardiovascular training mixes in endurance exercises with shorter workouts.

THE 12-WEEK TRAINING PROGRAM

This 12-week training program, designed to get you started on the road to your longevity goals, is divided into three phases (each consisting of a four-week block). Each phase is divided into three routines (A, B and C), along with a warm-up sequence. (The warm-up is very versatile, and you can incorporate it before any work-out, cardio session, sport activity or any other physical activities you're into.) Each four-week phase has its own schedule on the following pages.

I've designed the program with efficiency in mind, so you can adapt it to your schedule and get the most out of your day. Many of the exercises require only your body weight as resistance. Other exercises require a very small amount of basic equipment – kettlebells and dumbbells – so you can easily train at home or any gym you might belong to. Each routine contains only six exercises, to be done in pairs with a period of rest in between.

The warm-up will take only 5–10 minutes, and with the routine and short cardio elements included, the whole commitment takes between 45 and 75 minutes (max). You can do it!

The program is designed to be balanced, and it addresses a wide variety of common ailments that grow more severe as you age: knee pain, lower back pain, hip tightness, shoulder tightness. It also targets areas of the body crucial for sporting performance and general range of motion.

The tempo refers to the pace and intensity of effort – sometimes, just slow breathing, in other cases, it indicates the pacing or cadence sequence through the full range of motions in the exercise. For example, a squat with a 2-1-2 tempo means taking 2 seconds to go from a standing position to a squatting position, holding the squat for 1 second, then taking 2 seconds to press back up to a standing position.

KEY

SB = Swiss ball

DB = Dumbbells

KB = Kettlebell

SC = Short cardio, best done at the end of a session

LC = Long cardio, best for free days

BJJ = Brazilian jiu-jitsu

PHASE 1: RESET AND REHAB

WARM-UP SEQUENCE

EXERCISE	REPS	SETS	TEMPO	WEIGHT	REST
Supine diaphragmatic breathing	20	1	Slow breathing	Body	No
Pendulum walk	20 total	1	Slow and flowing, connected movements	Body	No
Elephant walk	30 steps	1	Slow/Flow	Body	No
Scorpion walk	12	1	Slow/Flow	Body	No
Dive jump	10	1	Slow/Flow	Body	No
Forward/ backward crawl	30 steps	1	Slow/Flow	Body	No
90/90 roll	16 total	2	Slow/Flow	Body	30 secs

ROUTINE A

EXERCISE	REPS	SETS	TEMPO	WEIGHT	REST
SB Superman deadlift	12–15	3–4	2 – 0 – 2	Body	
SB kneel	60–90 secs	3–4	1 – 0 – 1		60 secs
Rest before next exercise combo					*3–5 mins*
SB wall squat with bands	12–15	3	2 – 0 – 2	Body Medium– heavy bands	
BJJ hip mobility	12 total	3	2 – 0 – 2	Body	60 secs
Rest before next exercise combo					*3 mins*
Single leg wall hip thruster	15 each side	3	2 – 0 – 2	Body/ 10 kg	
SB dead bug	10 total	3	Slow breathing	Body	60 secs

ROUTINE B

EXERCISE	REPS	SETS	TEMPO	WEIGHT	REST
Bar hang	30 secs	3–4	Hold	Body	
Straight-arm plank	30 secs	3–4	Hold	Body	60 secs
Scapula push-up	20	3–4	Flow	Body	None – finish and start combo again
Rest before next exercise combo					*3 mins*
Straight-arm, straight-leg CHEK press (contralateral)	12	3	3 – 1 – 3	3–6 kg	
SB pullover (incline to flat)	12	3	2 – 0 – 2	3–6 kg	60 secs
Rest before next exercise combo					*3 mins*
SB straight-leg wood chop	12	3	2 – 1 – 1	5–8 kg	
Side plank with arm and leg counter rotation	12–15	3	2 – 0 – 2	Body	60 secs

ROUTINE C

EXERCISE	REPS	SETS	TEMPO	WEIGHT	REST
SB eccentric fly, concentric press	12	3	2 – 0 – 2	6–12 kg	
SB prone DB delt raise	12	3	3 – 0 – 3	2 – 5 kg	60 secs
Rest before next exercise combo					*3 mins*
Static box lunges with a stick	12 each leg	3	2 – 0 – 2	Body	
Single-leg SB wall squat	10 each leg	3	2 – 0 – 2	Body	60 secs
Rest before next exercise combo					*3–5 mins*
BJJ roll (with Swiss ball)	10	3	2 – 0 – 0	Body	
Reverse crunch	10–12	3	3 – 0 – 3	Body	75 secs

PHASE 1 SCHEDULE

	WEEK 1	WEEK 2	WEEK 3	WEEK 4
MONDAY	A SC	A	B	C SC
TUESDAY		B SC	C SC	B SC
WEDNESDAY	B SC	SC	SC	
THURSDAY		C SC	A	A SC
FRIDAY	C	A	C SC	C
SATURDAY	LC	LC	LC	LC
SUNDAY				

PHASE 2: REHAB TO STRENGTH

WARM-UP SEQUENCE

EXERCISE	REPS	SETS	TEMPO	WEIGHT	REST
Supine diaphragmatic breathing (legs up)	20	1	Breathe	Body	No
Pendulum walk	16 total	1	Slow/ controlled	Body	No
Pigeon walk	12 total	1	Slow	Body	No
Elephant walk	30 steps	1	Flow	Body	No
Scorpion walk	12	1	Flow	Body	No
Dive jump	12	1	Flow	Body	No
The lizard	12	1	Flow	Body	No

ROUTINE A

EXERCISE	REPS	SETS	TEMPO	WEIGHT	REST
KB single-leg deadlift	10	3–4	2 – 1 – 2	8–12 kg	
SB kneeling balance (with arms)	60–90 secs	3–4	Hold and play	Body	60–90 secs
Rest before next exercise combo					*3–5 mins*
SB KB wall squat	10	3	2 – 0 – 2	10–20 kg	
BJJ hip mobility (with weight)	12	3	2 – 0 – 2	8–12 kg	60 secs
Rest before next exercise combo					*3 mins*
SB reverse back extension	10–12	3	3 – 0 – 3	Body	
SB prone jackknife	8–10	3	3 – 1 – 3	Body	60–90 secs

ROUTINE B

EXERCISE	REPS	SETS	TEMPO	WEIGHT	REST
Ring pull-ups	10	3–4	2 – 0 – 2	Body	
Kneeling dive	10	3–4	2 – 0 – 2	Body	
Shoulder dislocates (with band or stick)	10	3–4	2 – 0 – 2	Body	None – finish and start combo again
Rest before next exercise combo					*3–5 mins*
Single-arm KB floor press	10–12	3	2 – 0 – 2	8–12 kg	
Cable wood chop (with pelvic shift)	10–12	3	2 – 0 – 2	12–18 kg	60 secs
Rest before next exercise combo					*3 mins*
Straight-arm forward SB roll	10	3	Slow	Body	
SB upper Russian twist	20 total	3	Slow/ breathe	3–5 kg med ball	60–90 secs

ROUTINE C

EXERCISE	REPS	SETS	TEMPO	WEIGHT	REST
Swimmer walk-outs	8–10	3	2 – 0 – 2	Body	
Single-leg cable external rotation	12	3	2 – 0 – 2	10 kg	60 secs
Rest before next exercise combo					*3–5 mins*
Lunging cable reverse wood chop	12	3	2 – 0 – 2 Remain stable	12–18 kg	
Multi-directional lunges	12 each side (4 points × 3)	3	Medium	Body	90 secs
Rest before next exercise combo					*3–5 mins*
BJJ roll (with SB)	12	3	Controlled	Body	
Medicine ball wall press	12	3	Timing	5–8 kg	60 secs

PHASE 2 SCHEDULE

	WEEK 5	WEEK 6	WEEK 7	WEEK 8
MONDAY	A SC	A SC	C SC	B SC
TUESDAY		C SC	B	C SC
WEDNESDAY	B SC			
THURSDAY	SC	B SC	C SC	A SC
FRIDAY	C	A	A	B
SATURDAY	LC	LC	LC	LC
SUNDAY				

PHASE 3: STRENGTH AND POWER

WARM-UP SEQUENCE

EXERCISE	REPS	SETS	TEMPO	WEIGHT	REST
Seated diaphragmatic breathing	20	1	Breathe	Body	No
Elephant walk	30 steps	1	Flow	Body	No
Scorpion walk	12	1	Flow	Body	No
Dive jump	12	1	Slow	Body	No
90/90 roll	20	2	Slow	Body	No
Sideways crawl	30 steps each side	1	Slow	Body	No
The lizard	12	1	Flow	Body	No

ROUTINE A

EXERCISE	REPS	SETS	TEMPO	WEIGHT	REST
Single-leg barbell deadlift	5–8	3–4	2 – 0 – 2	20–40 kg	
SB kneeling DB play (sagittal and transversal)	20–30	3–4	1 – 0 – 1	2–4 kg	90 secs
Rest before next exercise combo					*5 mins*
KB sumo squat		2–3	2 – 0 – 2		
4-point hip mobility (with twist)		2–3	2 – 0 – 2		60–90 secs
Rest before next exercise combo					*3–5 mins*
Supine lateral roll (with SB)	3–5 holds, 3 secs each	2–3	Slow/ controlled	Body	
SB prone jackknife	5–8	2–3	3 – 1 – 3	Body	90 secs

ROUTINE B

EXERCISE	REPS	SETS	TEMPO	WEIGHT	REST
Horizontal bar pull-up (feet on the bench)	6–10	3–5	3 – 0 – 3	Body	
Yoga block push-up	6–8	3–5	3 – 0 – 3	Body	
Table shoulder	10 10-sec hold	3–5	2 – 0 – 2	Body	90–120 secs
Rest before next exercise combo					*3–5mins*
Turkish get-up	5–8 each side	3		6–10 kg	
Swimmers	5	3	2 – 0 – 2	Tennis ball	60 sec
Rest before next exercise combo					*3–5 mins*
SB side plank	30–45 secs	3	2 – 0 – 2	Body	
Lower Russian twist (on floor)	12–16	3	2 – 0 – 2	3 kg medicine ball	90 secs

ROUTINE C

EXERCISE	REPS	SETS	TEMPO	WEIGHT	REST
Trap bar deadlift	10	4– 6	2 – 0 – 2	40–80 kg 70–80 per cent	90–120 secs
Rest before next exercise combo					*3–5 mins*
One arm, one leg DB reach extension (with rotation)	10	2–3	3 – 0 – 3	2–4 kg	
Horizontal cable wood chop (with forward lunges)	10 each side	2–3	2 – 0 – 2	12–16 kg	90 secs
Rest before next exercise combo					*3 mins*
Skate lunges	20–24 total	2–3	Slow slide	0–12 kg	60 secs
Rest before next exercise combo					*3 mins*
Single-leg cable reverse wood chop	12	2–3	2 – 0 – 2	18–25 kg	
Hip-hinge wall-ball press	12	2–3	2 – 0 – 2	5–10 kg	90 secs

PHASE 3 SCHEDULE

	WEEK 9	WEEK 10	WEEK 11	WEEK 12
MONDAY	A SC	A SC	B SC	C SC
TUESDAY		B	C SC	
WEDNESDAY	B SC	C SC		A SC
THURSDAY	SL	SL	A SC	B SC
FRIDAY	C SC	A SC	B	C
SATURDAY			LC	LC
SUNDAY				

12-WEEK PROGRAM, PHASE 1

PHASE 1: WARM-UP SEQUENCE

SUPINE DIAPHRAGMATIC BREATHING:

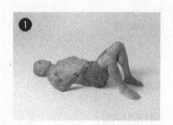

Lie on the floor on your back, legs bent at the knees with your feet flat on the floor. Place one hand on your belly and the other on your rib cage ❶. Inhale through your nose, expanding your belly first, then your rib cage, then your chest. Exhale.

PENDULUM WALK:

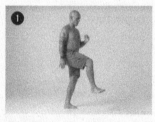

Walking in a straight line, bend your body forward (hip hinge) with one knee raised (like a single-leg deadlift) and arm hanging down at the same side ❶. As you step forward, plant that leg solidly on the ground and extend the other leg directly behind you, keeping it parallel to the floor with your back straight. Drop the arm on the same side as the straight leg, making a pendulum ❷. Keep moving forward step by step in this way for 20 reps.

ELEPHANT WALK:

In the downward-dog yoga pose (all fours with your arms and legs straight, and feet flat), take small steps to move forward, alternating hands and feet . Keep pushing your hands against the floor (at shoulder elevation) with each step . Don't allow your wrists, shoulders and hips to go out of alignment. Inhale and exhale on each step, for 20 reps.

SCORPION WALK:

On all fours, with your hands underneath your shoulders, arms straight, drive your right knee forward in a straight line, at an approximate angle of 45 degrees to the floor, keeping your left leg straight ❶. Place your right foot directly under your shoulders ❷. Keep focused on your hands: ensure your fingers are widely spread and that your weight is distributed evenly through the palms and the knuckles, particularly over the pointer and middle finger. Stretch your spine, forming a straight line between your hands, shoulders and hips. Once your spine is aligned, open your hip to the sky by swinging your right leg up and behind you, drawing your heel towards your glute so the leg remains bent ❸ ❹. Bring your right foot back between your hands and, in a flowing motion, shift your weight ahead and slide your hands forward. Repeat with the left leg ❺ then continue, changing from right to left leg, for 12 reps.

DIVE JUMP:

On all fours, with your hands underneath your shoulders and legs straight, dip and drive your head forward ❶, slowly moving your hips down to the floor ❷. Open your chest and squeeze your shoulder blades (for better stabilisation). Keep your head straight and look ahead ❷. Squeeze (activate) the glutes to release lower back tension ❸. Then bend your knees, push back to straighten your arms ❹ and settle into a squatting position ❺. Extend upwards and jump, landing back in the squat position. Try to sink as deeply into the squat as you can, to get the benefits of hip mobility ❻. Hold this position for 5 seconds before repeating (10 reps in all).

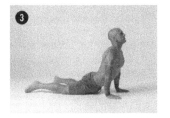

FORWARD/BACKWARD CRAWL:

Crawl forward, focusing on contralateral movement (right hand moves forward as left foot moves forward) and ensuring you don't raise one hip as you lift the opposite leg ❶. Keep your spine straight and elongated. Keep legs bent at a 90-degree angle. Move in small steps, and do not let your knee go past your belly button ❷. Move forward 15 steps before moving in the same way backwards for 15 steps.

90/90 ROLL:

Sit upright on the floor in the 90/90 position and inhale ❶. Slowly turn in the direction of the leg that's bent behind you ❷, exhaling, rolling both knees up until you're in a seated position, and then fold the knees through to the opposite side ❸. Use your hands as support if needed, until you get used to the rolling movement through the hips. Then try the roll without hand support ❹. Inhale at the start position and exhale when you are rolling.

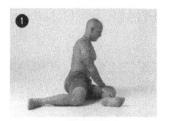

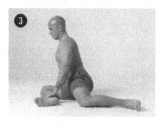

PHASE 1, ROUTINE A

SWISS BALL SUPERMAN DEADLIFT:
With a Swiss ball behind you, extend
your left leg behind you and place the
top of your left foot on top of the ball,
then extend your left arm away from
your chest ❶. Roll the ball back with
your foot and up the shin, bringing the
extended arm back and extending the
right arm instead ❷. Move to a hip-hinge
position. Try to keep your stability on your
right foot. Move the hip back towards
the starting position ❸. You will feel
your glutes activate and your ankles
shake on the baseline. You can use a
pole for balance ❹ ❺. Alternate legs
for 12–15 reps.

SWISS BALL KNEEL:

Place a Swiss ball close to the wall. Keeping yourself stable with one hand on the wall and the other on top of the ball, put one knee on top of the Swiss ball, followed by the other. Keep your knees apart, on the same line as your hips until you get your balance, then try widening your knees just a little more. This will activate your core. Continue to hold this position for 60–90 seconds. Remember: don't bend your hips and keep your spine straight and stiff. As you become more comfortable, try it without a hand on the wall ❶, and one or both arms extended forward.

SWISS BALL WALL SQUAT (WITH BANDS):

Place a belt or elastic strap around your legs at mid-thigh height. The belt should be tightened for support, so that you can hold a comfortable squat stance with your back against the wall without falling. Stand upright with a Swiss ball between your back and the wall. Inhale, then slowly lower yourself into a squat as you exhale . Go as low as you comfortably can , maintaining the arch in your lower back, then inhale as you return to the starting upright position . Breathe through your nose throughout the motion if you can. If not, exhale through your mouth.

BRAZILIAN JIU-JITSU HIP MOBILITY:

Kneel with your left leg bent behind you and your right leg bent in front at 90 degrees **1**. Sink your weight backwards and across your hips so your butt is closer to the floor, then step forward with the left leg **2**. The aim is to lift your hips from the floor so your knees come down on alternating sides. If you cannot get the needed lift in one motion, use a hand as support to help you through the movement. (The goal is to do it without hands.) A light kettlebell can be added for resistance, to further activate the core **3**. Complete 12 reps in total.

SINGLE-LEG WALL HIP THRUSTER:

Lie on your back and put one foot against the wall, knee bent at 90 degrees. Bend your toes up (dorsiflex) and press the heel into the wall. Extend your other leg straight up, with your sole to the ceiling ❶. With your arms extended on the floor for support, thrust your hip up, extending the straight leg further upwards ❷. The force will come from the heel. Exhale fast on the way up, and inhale slowly on the way down. You should feel the activation in your glutes. Complete 15 thrusts on each side ❸.

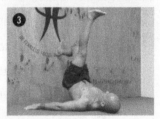

SWISS BALL DEAD BUG:

Lie down on the floor on your back, holding a Swiss ball between your hands and legs ❶. Drop one arm straight behind you while extending the opposite leg simultaneously. The foot and arm that stay on the ball will apply pressure, squeezing to keep it upright ❷. Exhale as you extend away from the Swiss ball and inhale as you bring your arm and leg back up into contact with it. Alternate for 10 total reps.

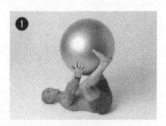
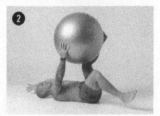

PHASE 1, ROUTINE B

BAR HANG:

Passively hang from a chin-up bar, palms out, and allow gravity to stretch yourself ❶. If it's hard for you initially, place some yoga blocks (or similar) under your feet to support and minimise your weight. Hold for 30 seconds ❷.

STRAIGHT-ARM PLANK:

Get into a push-up position, with arms straight and locked at the elbow. Press the floor, protracting your shoulder blades (scapulas), tucking your bottom in and locking the knees ❶. Hold for 30 seconds.

SCAPULA PUSH-UP:

From a 4-point position (the crawling position), make sure your hands and arms are in alignment with your shoulders ❶. Keep your spine straight and long (parallel to the floor), isolating the thoracic area and engaging the shoulder blades (scapulas). Push your scapulas towards the ceiling ❷ and then pull them towards the floor ❸ (protraction and retraction), inhaling when you retract and exhaling when you protract. Remember not to bend your elbows during the movement, and to keep your lower back still and stable. Complete 20 reps.

STRAIGHT-ARM, STRAIGHT-LEG CHEK PRESS (CONTRALATERAL):

Stand with your right leg raised, knee bent, and hold a dumbbell in your right hand up at ear height and at right angles to your body ❶. Rotate your wrist so your palm is facing forward, activate your core and push up the weight to arm's length above your head ❷. At the top, turn your arm and dumbbell back to a right angle to your body and lower the weight to shoulder height. Maintain good posture throughout the movement for 12 reps each side.

SWISS BALL PULLOVER (INCLINE TO FLAT):

Lie on a Swiss ball so that your head, shoulders and upper back are supported by the ball, with your hips dropped. Hold a dumbbell with both hands at arm's length overhead ❶. Lower the dumbbell towards the ground behind your head ❷. Raise your hips as you press the dumbbell back overhead ❸. Lower your hips to the start position ❹, and repeat for 12 reps.

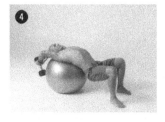

SWISS BALL STRAIGHT-LEG WOOD CHOP:

Sit on a Swiss ball and hold a dumbbell with both hands at your left hip with your left hand on top of your right one . Activate your core, lift your right leg off the floor and raise the dumbbell across your body diagonally towards the ceiling . Slowly lower and repeat for 12 reps before swapping sides .

SIDE PLANK WITH ARM AND LEG COUNTER-ROTATION:

Lie on your right side, legs extended and stacked from hip to feet. The elbow of your right arm should be directly under your shoulder ❶. Ensure your head is directly in line with your spine ❷. Your left arm should be aligned along the left side of your body. Activate your core, maintain a good posture and rotate your left arm and leg across your body in a counter-rotation ❸: as your left leg rotates forward, your left arm goes backwards, in a scissor motion. Next, bring your left arm in front of you as you move your left leg behind ❹.

Repeat for 12 reps ❺ before swapping to lie on your left side and repeating steps 1–5 but with your rights arm and leg.

PHASE 1, ROUTINE C

SWISS BALL ECCENTRIC FLY, CONCENTRIC PRESS:

Lie on a Swiss ball so that your head, shoulders and upper back are supported and your hips are raised. Hold two dumbbells at arm's length above your chest ❶. Lower the weights in a wide arc on either side, maintaining a slight bend in your elbow ❷. Bend your elbows to bring the weights into a press position at your shoulders ❸. Straighten your elbows and press the weights back above your chest. Repeat for 12 reps ❹.

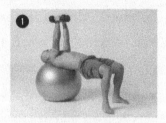

SWISS BALL PRONE DUMBBELL DELT RAISE:

Lying face-down over a Swiss ball with your chest on the ball and feet wide on the floor, hold two dumbbells with your thumbs facing inwards ❶. Activate your core and raise the dumbbells to either side until they are at shoulder height ❷, keeping your head and chest still ❸. Slowly lower the dumbbells to the start position, and repeat for 12 reps ❹.

STATIC BOX LUNGES WITH A STICK:

Start in a splits stance, with your front foot on a step box (or similar), holding a stick to one side for support ❶. Activate your core and lower into a lunge ❷, going as deep as possible while maintaining an upright spine ❸. Push off the box to rise to the start position. Perform 12 reps with each leg ❹.

SINGLE-LEG SWISS BALL WALL SQUAT:

Stand upright on your right leg with your left hip pinning a Swiss ball against the wall ❶. Raise your left knee slightly so your left foot is raised off the floor ❷. Place your right hand on your right hip, with your thumb monitoring the contraction of your glute. Maintaining an upright trunk and level pelvis, push sideways into the ball, then bend your right knee to lower your body. Keep your knee tracking over your second toe, and maintain sidewards pressure through the motion to keep the Swiss ball against the wall. Push up to straighten your knee and rise to the start position. Repeat for 10 reps on each side.

BRAZILIAN JIU-JITSU ROLL
(WITH SWISS BALL):

Lie on your back with a Swiss ball
between your raised arms and
legs ❶. Put pressure on the ball to
create a solid foundation ❷. Roll slowly
from side to side with your entire body
(head included), staying in control of
the movement and maintaining the
posture ❸. Do not drop to the floor or
lose attachment with the ball. You will
increase the range of movement the
more you are able to maintain this solid
control. Repeat for 12 reps.

REVERSE CRUNCH:

Lying on your back with your arms on the floor beside you, raise your feet off the floor ❶. Slowly bend your knees, thighs vertical ❷. Draw your belly button inwards, lift your pelvis off the floor and curl your spine ❸, peeling off the floor vertebrae by vertebrae. Use as little movement at your hips as possible ❹. Lower your legs in a controlled manner to the start position, and repeat for 10–12 reps.

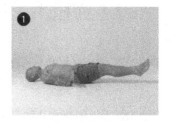

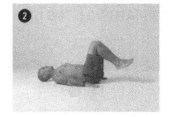

12-WEEK PROGRAM, PHASE 2

PHASE 2: WARM-UP SEQUENCE

SUPINE DIAPHRAGMATIC BREATHING (LEGS UP):

This is the same exercise as in Phase 1, except with both legs lifted off the floor, knees bent ❶ ❷.

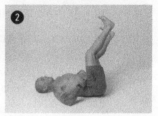

PENDULUM WALK: See description from Phase 1, page 108.

PIGEON WALK:

From a standing position, raise one leg up, open the hips and cross the foot across the other knee ❶. Squat down into this posture on the other leg, deepening the stretch into your hip ❷. Rise up, release the foot and step forward. Bring the other leg forward and repeat the motion ❸ ❹, alternating sides for 12 total reps.

ELEPHANT WALK: See description from Phase 1, page 109.

SCORPION WALK: See description from Phase 1, page 110.

DIVE JUMP: See description from Phase 1, page 111.

THE LIZARD:

From a straight-arm side plank, cross the top leg in front so your foot is pointing away from your body at 90 degrees (with your knee at 90 degrees too) **1**. At the same time, bring the top arm forward in a swimming motion and place it about 30 cm ahead of your other hand **2**. Move your back foot to where your support hand was, rotating to the other side **3**. Repeat the steps in small increments, for 12 total reps **4 5 6 7**. This flowing, simultaneous movement of your feet and hands will engage the core.

PHASE 2, ROUTINE A

KETTLEBELL SINGLE-LEG DEADLIFT:

Stand with your feet together in front of a kettlebell and then step your right leg behind you, big toe touching the floor for support. Lift the kettlebell with your right hand 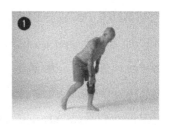. Hinge forward at the hips, continuing to hold the kettlebell, maintaining a straight arm (but don't touch the floor). Move your hips forward and bring your body back to the starting position . Inhale on your way down and exhale on your way up. Complete 10 reps on each side  .

SWISS BALL KNEELING BALANCE (WITH ARMS):

This exercise involves balancing on top of a Swiss ball on your knees, as in Phase 1, but with as little support as possible. (Make sure you are in a safe area.) Place your hands on top of the Swiss ball, and put one knee at a time near your hands. Find your balance. Stay close to the wall for support if it's still difficult. Don't be shy — use whatever you have to use to make your foundation solid. Hold this position for 60–90 seconds, raising your arms in front of you  or alternating raising each arm out and across your body for a deeper core workout  .

SWISS BALL KETTLEBELL WALL SQUAT:

Standing upright with a Swiss ball between your back and the wall, hold a kettlebell with two hands against your chest ❶. Activate your core and bend your knees to lower yourself into a squat ❷. Go as low as you comfortably can, maintaining the arch in your lower back, then push with your legs to return to the starting position. Repeat for 10 reps.

BRAZILIAN JIU-JITSU HIP MOBILITY (WITH WEIGHT):

Sit cross-legged then raise up your left leg, bending the knee at 90 degrees so the sole of your foot is flat on the ground. Hold a kettlebell with two hands against your chest ❶. The aim is to lift your hips from the floor so you're in a kneeling position, maintaining a straight back at all times ❷. Swap your legs around and repeat ❸. Complete 12 reps on each side.

SWISS BALL REVERSE BACK EXTENSION:

Lie face-down over a Swiss ball, with the ball positioned just below your chest, raise your legs in the air behind you ❶. Bring your heels together, pointing your toes ❷. Tighten your hamstrings and glutes, and hold this position for 2–3 seconds before lowering your legs again ❸. Complete 10–12 reps.

SWISS BALL PRONE JACKKNIFE:

In a push-up position, place your feet on the top of a Swiss ball ❶. Activate your core, draw your knees towards your chest so you drag the Swiss ball towards yourself without letting your hips drop, and maintain good postural alignment ❷. Keep the natural arch in your lower back. Slowly extend your legs and return to the starting position. Complete 8–10 reps.

PHASE 2, ROUTINE B

RING PULL-UPS:

Stand in front of the rings with your feet shoulder-width apart and adjust them to hang at chest level. Grasp the rings, palms down, and drop your body backwards to a 45-degree angle, lifting the soles of your feet up and pivoting on your ankles, keeping your arms straight with knees locked and activated gluteus ❶. Don't bend your head forward; maintain a straight neck. Inhale in this position, then adjust your hands in an external rotation so your palms and fingers face upwards, and exhale as you slowly pull yourself upwards to a standing position with scapulas engaged and elbows by your sides ❷. A more difficult variation is to lean further back to increase the angle to pull yourself up from. Repeat for 10 reps.

KNEELING DIVE:

Get into a 4-point position: knees wide open, on your toes, hands a little bit forward from your shoulders 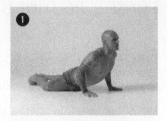. Drive your head down and forward, trying to touch your chest to the floor. At the same time, pull with your arms, moving your head past your hands then pushing up 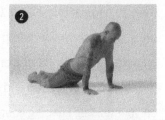. This will lift your upper body off the floor while your hips and legs flatten. The whole sequence is a wave-like motion through the spine. Lift your hips into the cat yoga pose (4-point position with arched back) , and then return to the starting position. Inhale when you are going forward, and exhale when you are moving back into the starting position. Complete 10 reps.

SHOULDER DISLOCATES (WITH BAND OR STICK):

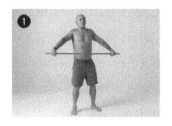

Standing upright with good posture, hold a stick parallel to the ground in both hands ❶. Activate your core, then exhale and raise the stick overhead and behind your back to stretch your chest and shoulders ❷. Repeat the same motion to bring the stick back over your head and in front. Move your hands a little closer together and repeat. Continue to perform the movement, moving your hands a little closer each time until you're just comfortable enough to perform the exercise. If the movement is difficult for you, use an elastic band instead. Complete 10 forward/backward reps.

SINGLE-ARM KETTLEBELL FLOOR PRESS:

Lying on your back on the floor, hold a kettlebell vertically from the bottom in the palm of one hand ❶. Press the weight to arm's length overhead ❷, then slowly return your elbow to the floor. Let the arm rest for a couple seconds before starting the next repetition. Complete 10–12 reps.

CABLE WOOD CHOP
(WITH PELVIC SHIFT):

Set the cable at just above head height. Stand with your feet a comfortable distance apart, with 70 per cent of your weight on the foot closest to the cable machine, knee slightly bent. Hold the cable handle with the hand furthest away from the cable column, and place the other hand over the top . Activate your core  and rotate your torso away from the cable machine while simultaneously pulling the handle down across your body and shifting your weight to the opposite foot , lunging laterally as you move . Slowly return to the starting position, and complete 10–12 reps.

STRAIGHT-ARM FORWARD SWISS BALL ROLL:

Hold a push-up position, with your hands on top of a Swiss ball ❶. Keep your navel and spine in a neutral position. Hold the alignment for 30 seconds while rolling the ball forward and backwards.

SWISS BALL UPPER RUSSIAN TWIST:

Lie on a Swiss ball in a bridge position, with your upper back resting on the ball and your feet on the floor. Place your palms together and extend your arms fully out in front from your chest ❶. Activate your core, and twist your upper body side to side ❷ ❸, rolling across your shoulders. Complete 20 side-to-side reps.

PHASE 2, ROUTINE C

SWIMMER WALK-OUTS:

Standing with your feet a comfortable distance apart, bend forward from the hips and place your hands on the ground ❶. Slowly walk your hands out (keeping your feet planted) and lower your body ❷. Keep your body rigid and walk out only as far as you comfortably can. Walk your hands back in, raising your body to its standing position. Complete 8–10 reps.

SINGLE-LEG CABLE EXTERNAL ROTATION:

Set the cable at just above head height. Standing on one leg (the one closest to the cable machine), hold the cable across your body with your opposite hand, as if reaching into your pocket. Activate your core and pull your arm up and across your body ❶, rotating the arm so the thumb faces up at the top of the movement ❷ ❸. Lower slowly, and repeat for 12 reps.

LUNGING CABLE REVERSE WOOD CHOP:

Set the cable as close to the floor as possible. Stand with your feet a comfortable distance apart and raise one knee to waist height ❶. Hold the cable handle with the hand furthest from the cable column and place your other hand over the top, arms extended straight from the chest ❷. Activate your core and rotate your torso away from the cable machine while simultaneously pulling the handle up across your body up the opposite shoulder ❸. Slowly return to the starting position, and repeat for 12 reps.

MULTI-DIRECTIONAL LUNGES:

Begin each part of the exercise standing upright with feet shoulder-width apart and pointing forward. You can hold a stick behind your back as shown to make sure your posture is upright through the movement. Each leg will be lunging in five different directions.

Front lunge: Step straight forward in the 'noon' direction with your right foot, keeping your chest upright, so that your left knee touches the ground ❶ ❷. Push back into the starting position.

Front 45-degree lunge: Step halfway between noon and 3 o'clock (right leg) ❸ or noon and 9 o'clock (left leg), depending on which foot you're stepping with. Your head and eyes should face forward, and your pelvis and shoulders should be square to the front. Allow the back leg to pivot naturally as you lower into the lunge ❹. (Do not turn the whole body 45 degrees, as that wouldn't be any different than the front lunge.)

Lateral lunge: Step out to the side at 3 or 9 o'clock, depending on which foot you're stepping with. Both feet should be facing forward; bend the leg you step out with.

Back 45-degree lunge: Step backwards between 3 and 6 o'clock or 6 and 9 o'clock, depending on which foot you're stepping with. Keep your body facing forward as you step backwards, with the back foot facing about 45 degrees inwards. Lower the back knee until it just touches the ground.

Back lunge: Step directly backwards to 6 o'clock behind you; the rear knee should touch the ground.

Complete 15 lunges with each leg (three steps in each of the five directions).

BRAZILIAN JIU-JITSU ROLL (WITH SWISS BALL):
See description from Phase 1, page 128.

MEDICINE BALL WALL PRESS:
Kneel on both knees in front of the wall with your hips raised, and hold a medicine ball in front of your chest ❶. Power press (throw) the ball against the wall, catching it on the rebound ❷. Repeat action for 12 reps.

12-WEEK PROGRAM, PHASE 3

PHASE 3: WARM-UP SEQUENCE

SEATED DIAPHRAGMATIC BREATHING:

Sit cross-legged on the floor with your back straight. Take a slow, deep breath, expanding your abdominal wall as you inhale ❶. As you exhale, allow your abdominal wall to sink back. Relax into 20 breaths ❷. A more challenging variation is to sit on a Swiss Ball while you do this breathing exercise.

ELEPHANT WALK: see description from Phase 1, page 109.

SCORPION WALK: see description from Phase 1, page 110.

DIVE JUMP: see description from Phase 1, page 111.

90/90 ROLL: see description from Phase 1, page 53.

SIDEWAYS CRAWL:

From a 4-point position, move sideways by alternately bringing your hands together while your feet are apart, and vice versa – as you move, your arms will be close together and your legs will be apart ❶. Keep your spine elongated and crawl in a slow, controlled manner for 30 steps on each side.

THE LIZARD: see description from Phase 2, page 132.

PHASE 3, ROUTINE A

SINGLE-LEG BARBELL DEADLIFT:
Standing on your left leg, reach down
and grab a barbell with both hands at
slightly more than shoulder-width apart,
keeping the natural arch in your lower
back ❶. Raise your chest, look forward
and inhale, drawing your belly button
inwards. Bend forward slightly until the
bar is at knee level ❷. Lift your torso as
high as you can, exhaling through pursed
lips through the most challenging point
of the movement. Imagine trying to push
the ground away from you with your left
foot. At the top, inhale before lowering
the bar back to the ground. Repeat for
5–8 reps on each leg.

SWISS BALL KNEELING DUMBBELL PLAY (SAGITTAL AND TRANSVERSAL):

Kneeling on a Swiss ball, hold one dumbbell at your side **❶**. Activate your core and raise the dumbbell in an arc **❷ ❸ ❹** until it is at shoulder height in front of you, maintaining balance on the ball **❺**. Bring your hands together in front of your chest, pass the dumbbell into your other hand and then move your arms back out to your sides. Repeat, swapping hands in front of your chest on each repetition, for 20–30 reps.

KETTLEBELL SUMO SQUAT:

Start with a wide stance, feet pointed 45° out. Squat down and grab two kettlebells from between your feet , keeping a neutral spine, navel in and shoulder blades squeezed together . Extend your knees, breathing in , until you're fully upright . Squat back down, breathing out. Complete 10–12 reps.

4-POINT HIP MOBILITY (WITH TWIST):

Sit on the floor, forming 90-degree angles with each knee, both feet pointing to the right. Place your right knee close to the sole of your left foot, pushing it forward ❶. Lift yourself up on top of the knee and ankle joints ❷. Rotate your body, twisting your trunk around to the right ❸. Make sure your glutes touch the floor as you rotate, and lift again as you come back to the original position ❹ ❺. Ensure your core is activated through the whole movement. A good start is to try 10 reps and hold for 10 secs.

SUPINE LATERAL ROLL
(WITH SWISS BALL):

Roll back on a Swiss ball until the ball supports your head, shoulders and upper back. Lift your hips until they are level with your knees and shoulders ❶. Maintain this alignment as you shuffle your feet and roll across the ball to one side. Pause for 3 seconds, and return to the centre, before moving to the other side. Move only as far as you comfortably can to each side while maintaining good alignment (hips and arms parallel to the floor). You may only be able to move an inch or two, which is fine. Complete 3–5 reps.

PRONE JACKKNIFE
(WITH SWISS BALL):

Get into a push-up position with your feet on a Swiss ball ❶. Draw your belly button inwards, push with your hands to raise your chest while drawing your feet towards your chest so your body and legs make a Z shape ❷. Maintain a good postural alignment – a natural arch in your lower back and hips elevated – for 1 second. Roll your feet back in a controlled motion so you're in the starting position. Repeat for 5–8 reps.

PHASE 3, ROUTINE B

HORIZONTAL BAR PULL-UP
(FEET ON THE BENCH):

Lie face-up below a bar set to a little higher than arm's length above the floor. Hold the bar (overhand grip) with straight arms while your feet rest on a low bench ❶. Activate your core, keeping your body aligned, and pull with your arms to bring your chest to the bar ❷. Lower yourself in a controlled motion, for 6–10 reps.

YOGA BLOCK PUSH-UP:

Position two yoga blocks (or similar) under your hands, just outside of shoulder-width, and get into a push-up position ❶. Drop your chest, trying to touch it to the floor. The main goal it is to improve the range of motion beyond a traditional push-up ❷ ❸ ❹ ❺. If this is hard for you, start on your knees for a couple of sessions before moving to straight knees ❻ ❼ ❽. Complete 6–8 reps.

TABLE SHOULDER: See description from Morning Routine, page 55.

TURKISH GET-UP:

Lying on your back on the floor, bend one knee and place your foot flat on the floor while extending the other leg. Hold a single kettlebell at arm's length above your shoulder ❶. Activate your core and perform a sit-up while holding the kettlebell overhead, using your opposite arm for assistance ❷.

Push off your grounded foot and thrust your hips forward to come to a standing position ❸ ❹ ❺ ❻. Reverse the movements, lowering in a controlled motion, until you're back in the starting position. Switch the kettlebell to the other side and repeat. Complete 5–8 reps each side.

SWIMMERS:

Lie face-down on the floor with a yoga block (or similar) under each elbow. Place your hands on top of your head for the starting position ❶. Lift your elbows up, straightening your arms forward before moving them back behind you in an internal rotation. Bend them at the back as you place your hands on your lower back ❷. Stop there, rest for 3–5 seconds, then move your hands in an external rotation until you've returned to the starting position ❸ ❹. (Only rest when your hands are at the back.) Complete 5 reps.

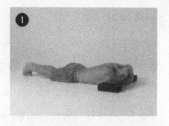

SWISS BALL SIDE PLANK:

Lie in a raised side-plank position with your body weight on one forearm on top of a Swiss ball ❶. If you find this too difficult, rotate the top leg forward (bent at the knee) for support ❷. Reach upwards with the other arm. Activate your core and lift your hips to form a straight line with your neck, sternum, belly button and knee. Maintain this position for 5 seconds, lower and repeat for 8 reps on each side.

LOWER RUSSIAN TWIST (ON FLOOR):

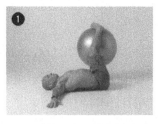

Lie on your back with arms stretched out at shoulder height, palms up with your hips bent to 90 degrees and legs as straight as possible. Activate your core and twist your trunk to the side as you lower your legs towards the floor, then use your abdominals to twist your lower body back to the start. Swap to the opposite side and repeat twisting from one side to the other for 12–16 reps. (For a deeper core workout, hold a Swiss ball between your legs through the motion, as shown ❶ ❷.)

PHASE 3, ROUTINE C

TRAP BAR DEADLIFT:

Standing with your feet a comfortable width apart inside the diamond of a trap bar, reach down and grab the bar handles ❶. Inhale, activate your core, pick your chest up and pull a curve into your lower back. Squeeze your shoulder blades together, drive with your legs to lift the bar off the floor ❷, then extend your hips to stand upright. Exhale through pursed lips through the most challenging point of the movement. Lower the weight in a controlled motion, and repeat for 10 reps.

ONE ARM, ONE LEG DUMBBELL REACH EXTENSION (WITH ROTATION):

Stand on one leg, holding a light dumbbell in the opposite hand. Activate your core and bend forward at the hip while reaching your dumbbell arm down below your chest ❶. Keep this range of motion comfortable throughout. Return to the upright position while raising the dumbbell and rotating your arm to shoulder height with the elbow bent up at 90 degrees ❷. Complete 10 reps on each side.

HORIZONTAL CABLE WOOD CHOP (WITH FORWARD LUNGES):

Set the cable at just above head height. Standing with your feet a comfortable distance apart, hold the cable handle with the hand furthest away from the cable column and place your other hand over the top. Activate your core, lunge forward and drop down as far as you comfortably can ❶. At the same time, rotate your torso away from the cable machine while pulling the handle horizontally across your body ❷. Slowly push back on your front leg and return to the starting position. Repeat for 10 reps on each side.

SKATE LUNGES:

Position your feet in a wide stance.
Activate your core and bend at your
knees into a deep squat, then shift your
weight to one side in a lateral lunge so
one leg is extended out to the side ❶.
Keeping your hips low, shift your weight
to the opposite side ❷. Repeat the lateral
sliding movement for 20–24 reps. (You
can add load by holding a dumbbell with
both hands at the centre of your chest.)

SINGLE-LEG CABLE REVERSE WOOD CHOP:

Set the cable as close to the floor as
possible. Stand on the leg that's closest
to the cable machine and hold the cable
handle with the hand furthest away from
it, with your other hand over the top ❶.
Activate your core and your spine, and
rotate your torso away from the cable
column while simultaneously pulling the
handle upwards across your body ❷.
Keep your hips facing forward ❸. Slowly
return to the start, and repeat for 12 reps
each side.

HIP-HINGE WALL-BALL PRESS:

Kneeling in front of a wall, sit back on your heels with a medicine ball raised to your chest. Hinge forward at your hips and power press (throw) the ball towards the wall, extending your arms fully. Catch the ball and sink back to the starting position, keeping the medicine ball raised. Repeat for 12 reps.

4.
NOURISH YOUR BODY

'Nourish your body.' It's something everyone loves talking about. Who doesn't enjoy a nice meal? But you also hear, 'Your body is your temple; you must take care of it.' But these things aren't mutually exclusive: you can nourish your body *without* wrecking the temple! Giving your body the proper nutrients, through the proper foods, is essential to optimal performance, gut health and so much more. Most importantly, it's one of the pillars of longevity.

We need food to survive – and it also plays a big part in our enjoyment of life – but we all define 'food' differently. As I said earlier, instead of going on a crash diet, it is much better for us to educate ourselves about what quality food really is, and understand exactly what we're putting in our mouths. We're not talking about restricting calories; we're investigating the *quality* of those calories.

Before we get into the detail of nutrition, here are a few things to keep in mind:

PRIORITISE NUTRIENT-DENSE FOODS

Your food should be rich in micronutrients, such as vitamins, minerals and antioxidants. These nutrients protect your body from cellular damage and inflammation which are linked to chronic diseases, such as cancer, diabetes and heart disease. As a general rule, include plenty of fruits, vegetables, lean proteins (eggs, tofu, fish, chicken breast, grass-fed beef) and whole grains (brown rice, quinoa, oats) to ensure you're getting a wide variety of micronutrients.

HYDRATE, HYDRATE, HYDRATE

Water is *essential* for good health – and survival! It keeps you hydrated but also aids in digestion, regulates body temperature, and cushions your joints. Aim to drink at least eight to 12 glasses of water daily; more if you exercise a lot or live in a hot climate.

DON'T FEAR FATS

The right fats are an essential component of a healthy diet. Healthy fats, such as monounsaturated and polyunsaturated fats, help your body absorb essential vitamins and minerals, reduce inflammation and lower your risk of heart disease. Healthy sources of fats include avocados, nuts, olive oil and salmon.

MIND YOUR MICROBIOME

Your gut is home to hundreds of millions of bacteria that are critical to your overall health. This group of microscopic organisms is known collectively as your 'microbiome'. A healthy, well-balanced microbiome helps with weight loss, better immune function and less inflammation. In order to promote good gut health, eat various fibre-rich foods, such as fruits, vegetables and whole grains, and include probiotics, such as fermented foods, like kimchi and kefir.

BALANCE YOUR MACRONUTRIENTS

Macronutrients are the nutrients your body needs in bigger amounts, such as proteins, carbohydrates and fats. A well-balanced diet includes all three of these macronutrients. Proteins are essential for building and repairing tissues; carbohydrates are important for energy; and healthy fats are essential for proper metabolic function.

In the introduction I discussed my journey to better nutrition, trying different diets and playing around with various foods and supplements. Getting a blood test done gave me an accurate picture of my overall health. I learned which of my markers were down; which were up; and which medications might help me. I did a lot of damage to my gut as a kid taking courses of strong antibiotics. Luckily, my mum was Spanish, so most of the food that was cooked at home was Spanish food – fresh,

nutritious and healthy. Well, mostly! We did eat a lot of offal –
liver, brains, tongue, kidneys and tripe – the works. I hated it,
and every time I saw my mum cooking these organs I'd try to
run away. But we couldn't afford to waste a meal. I had to try
everything before I was allowed to leave the table. The fact is
that if kids aren't taught about correct nutrition, they're going to
eat rubbish most the time. It's human nature.

I now realise some of my health problems stemmed from
poor digestion and poor hydration (which might have been
related to taking so many antibiotics). It wasn't from eating junk
food in my case! And it wasn't from not eating any protein. It's
hard to say what was missing from my diet. My family had a
small farm that we would go to on the weekends, collecting
fresh vegetables, fresh milk and eggs, chickens and fruit. My
mum made fresh cheese from the three cows on the property, so
by a process of elimination, I think my digestive problems were
probably due to the antibiotics.

My parents' generation didn't eat junk food, or genetically
modified food, so they didn't suffer the other problems that can
arise due to industrialised food manufacturing. Everything they
ate was clean and organic. Their diet also consisted of fewer
grains and no added sugar. Before processed sugar arrived in
the 1500s, our ancestors ate honey, dates and fruit to get their
'sugar fix'. I feel lucky to be able to teach my daughter what
quality food is and how to eat like her ancestors. I'm already
seeing what a difference it's making in her development.

I later found out that I couldn't digest protein properly, that
I had too much unhealthy heliobacteria in my guts, low levels
of neutrophils (white blood cells that help fight bacteria and

infection), as well as an intolerance to dairy and eggs. After many years of being sleep deprived after working 12- to 16-hour days chasing my goals, my testosterone levels had plummeted.

What was the turning point? I quickly learned that acquiring as much data on yourself and your own unique chemical make-up is crucial to better health and longevity. And you can get this information pretty easily from your GP through blood, urine and stool tests. A lot of health professionals still recommend restrictive diets, but they don't always examine a person's specific needs. Food is medicine, but there's a lot of conflicting information out there on what's best for each individual.

Eating 'clean', organic and 'real' food is one of the best ways to support our overall health. Good nutrition helps us heal, fight illness and move well as we age. It protects our mental health against the stresses of life and makes us more energetic and alert. But to be clear, everyone's body is different; what my body loves in terms of frequency of meals, quantity and composition is likely different from what your body loves. Having said that, there are some basic guidelines that apply to pretty much everyone.

We generally function better eating three to five smaller meals a day, rather than one or two bigger meals, as it helps stabilise our blood sugar levels. I regularly practise intermittent fasting (16 hours max), and, once every two months, I do a 24-hour fast to completely reset and cleanse my system. I also try to eat lots of different coloured fruits and vegetables, as they offer a wide range of micronutrients (vitamins and minerals). Some people can tolerate high-grain diets; while others have no problem eating a lot of dairy. Designing the perfect diet for you and your body isn't easy! There are many factors to consider, so take your time, do your research, and work out what's best for you.

What is certain is that a healthy diet will allow you to maintain muscle mass and build strength. In order to do this, it is essential to monitor how much protein you eat. Many people suffer from protein deficiency because modern meals often contain too many carbohydrates and too little protein. Start a food diary and check how many carbs you are eating and compare that with your protein intake. The average person should eat 0.8 to 1 grams of protein per kilo of body weight each day. Everyone has different protein requirements, but 100 grams should be the goal for most people. You will need to eat more if you are a very active person or a competitive athlete – between 1.2 to 2 grams per kilo of body weight. Less active people can get by with less. I weigh around 76 kilos, and being very active, need to consume 1.5 to 2 grams of protein per kilogram of body weight, or around 150 grams daily.

My diet incorporates aspects of the Mediterranean and paleo diets and includes:

- A high proportion of plant-based foods, including vegetables, fruits, legumes, nuts, seeds, whole grains, herbs, spices and olive oil.
- Seafood and fish (fresh, sustainably caught).
- Red meat (organic, free-range and grass-fed).
- Japanese food is ideal for me as it typically includes a lot of fresh seafood, fish, rice, noodles, soup (broth) and vegetables.

I try to avoid eating the following:

- Dairy products (except for the occasional serve of goat's cheese).
- Pasta, pizza, white rice and bread. I do this mainly to cut down on my intake of gluten.
- Refined sugars.
- Eggs, because I've discovered I have an intolerance to them. I still have one every week without ill-effects, but the problems rear up when I have them more often.
- Cereals.
- Processed meats.

I have a slice or two of good sourdough or gluten-free bread every six weeks. I have a great woodfired pizza once every 8 to 10 weeks at a pizzeria I know well and where they use high-quality, super fresh produce. I eat white rice once every 2 to 3 weeks in my sushi, but if the restaurant has the option of sushi with brown rice, I will go with that, although generally I prefer sashimi and soups. If I eat chocolate, I go for 85 per cent cocoa dark chocolate or a vegan option. My weakness is ice cream! I love it, but I can only eat dairy-free (vegan option) ice cream because of my intolerance.

Your body won't work as well as it could if you eat exactly the same thing every single day, so try to rotate two to three different breakfasts, lunches, dinners and snacks a week to mix things up. Be creative and you'll soon start seeing results just by cutting back on some of the foods you know aren't healthy or cause a bad reaction, and replacing them with better quality options. Research conducted by the American College of Sports Medicine says plant-based diets high in unrefined organic foods are best for improving health, lifespan, immune function and cardiovascular health.

So, I hope you are now starting to appreciate the importance of balance and moderation when it comes to nutrition. Understand, respect and work out what is best for you and your body, and learn which bad habits need to be tackled! Don't be afraid to experiment with new foods and meal plans; sometimes you need a shake-up of your routine to find the best diet for you. Be curious about your body's chemistry, and be open to learning and trying new things.

Before you start a new nutrition plan, begin with an assessment of everything you put into your body. (You'll need to allow some time in your schedule to plan the adjustments you intend to make.) Depending on your level of activity and goals, I suggest trialling the new routine for at least two to four weeks. This doesn't mean depriving yourself of food or stopping having a good time; but rather including high-quality, fresh foods while avoiding unhealthy foods (junk food, fast food, sugary foods, processed foods) and beverages like alcohol and coffee. You could follow paleo or keto principles, or take a vegetarian or vegan approach, depending on who you are, what your body needs, what you enjoy and the specific goals you've set for yourself.

For example, I never stop eating carbs entirely. I try to find better quality carbs or high-quality fats to give me energy and help my body recover. I also eat a good amount of protein before and after training. But I don't eat processed pasta, bread, rice or other grains. If I can find an excellent gluten-free, vegan banana bread option, I might eat it after training or at dinnertime. Why? Carbohydrates at night suit the parasympathetic nervous system, that network of nerves that promotes relaxation after a period of stress or danger. It slows your heart and breathing rates, lowers your blood pressure and promotes digestion. The more time we spend in the parasympathetic stage, the healthier we will be. And carbs are a good way of achieving this.

The funny (and fun) thing is that the more you know about how your body works, what time of day to eat, your physiology and how and what exercises complement your nutrition plan, you will eat everything that you like at the right time and in the right way. Life becomes far more enjoyable than just avoiding those things that don't work for you or are nutritionally poor. For example, when you finish a hard workout session, you'll be able to eat a big tablespoon of honey, a raw vegan cake or some ice cream, maybe even some woodfired pizza. Why? Because you need to repair the muscle tissue damage you may have sustained from the workout and replenish the insulin you will have lost. It's fine to eat quality carbs, protein and healthy fats after a workout.

Human beings are 'flavour hunters'. We are always looking for satisfying tastes that might not be good for us, such as sugary and highly processed foods and sweets. The great thing is we can satisfy those urges by eating quality foods containing fresh and organic ingredients, and *natural* sugars. Some people don't live in an area where good quality, free range or organic food is accessible or affordable. I lived in London in 2004–2005 – a grey, cold place, where there is no shortage of fast food options and pubs – but by scouring the suburbs for organic markets and shops, I managed to find affordable fresh fruit and vegetables, fish, and chicken and meat. It wasn't always easy, but it *was* possible!

Most major supermarkets in our big cities these days offer a range of healthy organic options. In most cities and towns, you'll also find vegetarian restaurants, which usually place a great emphasis on quality produce. Check out your local area, try different products in your cooking, and bring on those new and better habits!

Why? Well, because it's hard to go wrong eating whole, unprocessed foods just as nature created them. The main trap that people fall into is eating things that are high in calories but low in nutrients. This is why, for me, it is essential to monitor the quality and quantity of food I eat before and after training, even when I break my fast, to ensure I have good nutrients and the right calories to recover, improve and keep me on the path to greater longevity.

ONE PER CENT IMPROVEMENT EACH DAY – NO EXCUSES!

Travel is one of my passions, and having a solid food foundation means I can adapt wherever I may be. If I'm on a surf trip on an isolated island, I'll try to eat seafood, fish, fruit, vegetables and any other type of carbs and protein that are available. While the source of those nutrients might change, most cultures recognise the importance of maintaining nutritional balance in their diet.

In addition to making wise food choices, I also supplement my diet with:

Creatine (3 to 5 grams per day): an amino acid that improves strength, helps retain water and maintains good hydration of the muscles. It's also another source of energy to fight fatigue, aids in muscle recovery, and is an essential brain compound to support and restore energy and oxygen levels.

EAAs (essential amino acids): these are necessary because your body doesn't produce them by itself. We must consume them via a special diet or supplements. They aid in muscle growth and help with recovery. Talk to your GP about them.

Super greens: a supplement that nourishes the gut in the morning with a good hit of antioxidants, prebiotics, anti-inflammatories and more.

Spirulina: this type of blue-green algae boasts antioxidants and anti-inflammatory properties, supports blood sugar control, promotes longevity, reduces blood pressure, is rich in vitamins and essential minerals to maintain a healthy immune system, boosts the production of white blood cells and antibodies that fight viruses and bacteria in your body, improves gut health and more.

Acetyl-L-carnitine (1 to 1.5 grams a day, best taken in the morning on an empty stomach): an amino acid found in nearly all cells in the body. It's also found in red meat and in smaller quantities in white meat (chicken and fish), milk, avocados and asparagus. Acetyl-L-carnitine helps metabolise fat into energy and in the functioning of cells in the central nervous system. It also helps improve memory, mental function, mood and energy delivery to the cells.

Zinc: a trace mineral, meaning the body only needs a small amount. I take 8 to 11 milligrams per day. Zinc is essential for developing cells, building proteins, healing damaged tissue and supporting a healthy immune system.

Magnesium citrate: essential to help muscles and nerves work properly and keeps blood sugar levels and blood pressure at a reasonable level. You can take it daily, but no more than 400 milligrams.

L-Glutamine: I take this essential amino acid to help my digestion and keep my gut lining healthy, particularly important given my past digestive problems. It also helps remove waste products from the body, boosts the immune system and aids in muscle recovery and brain function. We can usually produce enough glutamine if we have a proper diet, but it is sometimes helpful to augment it with supplements. Glutamine, as an amino acid, acts as a building block for making proteins in the body for muscle recovery. I take 5 grams every night before bed. Some research shows that it's okay to take it more often.

I keep protein powder supplements handy in case I need a meal replacement or if I want a smoothie; otherwise, I prefer my EAAs (essential amino acids).

First thing in the morning after my routine (generally 60 to 90 minutes after I wake up), I do the following:

- I mix my super greens (1 scoop) with 1 gram of L-carnitine, 5 grams of creatine and six spirulina tablets.
- I will take my EAAs if I'm going to surf or train early.

Before bed:

- I take zinc and magnesium.
- I then take my EAAs to help me recover.

I might take other supplements after one of my semi-regular blood tests, like vitamins B12, D and others if needed. I might also take beta-alanine to enhance my performance, increase my capacity during training and decrease muscle fatigue. It has anti-oxidants to enhance the immune system and has been shown to aid in longevity. I take only 1 to 3 grams daily. You can also get beta-alanine from 'carnosine' food like meat, chicken and turkey.

Those are the supplements I take, but yours will be different, depending on your body's needs, your deficiencies and your exercise load. Talk to your GP, nutritionist or naturopath about what's best for you.

I'm a very active person, training five to seven days a week – surfing, Brazilian jiu-jitsu, yoga, practising my movement, weight training – while also studying, writing and meditating. I have to balance the physical and mental, so I try to be smart with my day so my body doesn't break down and my mind doesn't get fatigued. After many years trialling lots of different types of supplements (and throwing a lot of money down the drain), I'm confident with what I take now, but the research never stops, and I'm always open to new ideas. You too should never stop learning what keeps you fit and healthy. If you stop, you limit yourself and your knowledge.

Again let me stress that before taking any supplements, talk to your GP, nutritionist or naturopath and consider doing a blood test. I like to check the following blood markers every six months:

- All hormone levels – testosterone, HGH, DHEA, cortisol and others (women can have the same tests related to them)
- Thyroid function
- Cholesterol levels
- Liver function
- Kidney function
- Essential vitamin levels.

Other tests I've taken less frequently, or only once as directed, include:

- Blood type test. (To know what your blood type is so you can research diets that you might respond better to.)
- Ancestral test (saliva). Confirming my genetic composition put me on the right pathway to try foods my ancestors might have eaten.
- Food allergy test. I knew I couldn't eat dairy or eggs, but after a few years of cleansing my system, I was able to go back to eating tiny amounts. Always know which kind of

farm or environment your produce is coming from (free-range, organic, etc.).

If it sounds like there's a lot that goes into setting up your own nutritional plan, you're right! As with any pursuit, knowledge is power, and that knowledge isn't always easily acquired. But we need this kind of fundamental understanding of our bodies, who we are on a chemical level, and under what conditions we're most likely to thrive. You don't just start a diet because someone you follow posted on social media and everyone else is jumping on board. It's essential to get some direction first. As I always say, it's best to be precise from the outset in order to put yourself on the right path to longevity.

If you want to do some or all of the tests I've mentioned above, make sure you talk to your GP or nutritionist. They'll prescribe them and help you take the first steps.

THE IMPORTANCE OF HYDRATION AND GUT HEALTH

We must not forget the most essential food in the world: water! Humans can survive two weeks in the desert without food, but they cannot survive three days without water. Why? Well, water is essential for many reasons:

- Delivers nutrients to cells
- Regulates body temperature
- Lubricates joints

- Prevents infections
- Lowers inflammation
- Improves sleep quality
- Improves cognition
- Improves mood
- Helps efficient digestion
- Promotes healing
- Improves brain performance (mild dehydration – even as little as a 2 per cent loss – can affect memory, mood, concentration and reaction time)
- Boosts energy levels and vitality
- Drives kidney function and flushes out waste and impurities from the body (detox)
- Contributes to heart health
- Assists in weight control
- Boosts skin health.

Fatigue is one of the first signs of dehydration. If you're feeling sluggish and tired by midday, you might not be drinking enough water. You need to start drinking water as soon as you wake up. When you're dehydrated, your heart has to work harder to pump oxygenated blood throughout your body. The same goes for the other organs – they work less efficiently when you're dehydrated. It's a simple concept, but curiously hard to follow!

When I ask my clients to drink more water, they complain about having to go to the toilet all the time – or they'll tell me about the colour of their urine! If you're going to the toilet all the time it means your body is trying to adapt to the amount of water you're drinking. If you drink the right amount, your other systems will regulate themselves. Soon you'll be a new you with a healthy new habit in your arsenal – one that's so easy to do. Generally speaking, the lighter the colour of your urine, the better hydrated you are.

So, if you're finding that little things are annoying you, making you tired or irritable, please grab a bottle of water, and *not* a sugary soft drink or even some fruit juices (which are often just sugary water with the fibre removed). Even the smallest imbalances can affect the way you function. I always keep a couple of bottles of water on my desk or beside me when I'm coaching to remind myself to hydrate throughout the day.

Poor sleep, headaches and migraines can also be triggered by dehydration. Studies published in the *European Journal of Neurology* show that drinking more water helps reduce the symptoms and frequency of headaches. When you start to get dehydrated, your brain shrinks slightly, which can affect short-term memory and mental clarity. The brain is a fatty organ and needs water to function correctly.

Hydration also affects your gut health and bowel motions. If you don't drink enough water, the colon pulls it from your stool, which can lead to discomfort and constipation. And while we all appreciate an ice-cold drink, *warm* water is actually much better for healthy digestion. It improves gut function by helping to break down your food properly.

Remember that when you eat a large meal, your gut will need *twice* as much water to digest and process the food. If you experience discomfort or constipation, think about eating smaller meals and drinking two to three glasses of water 10 to

15 minutes *before* your meal, and then two glasses 10 minutes *after* your meal.

But exactly *how much* water should you be drinking each day?

It varies from person to person, but I have a simple formula: take your body weight in kilograms and multiply that number by 0.033, and you'll get the rough amount of water you should be drinking during a normal day in litres. (If you are training, or it's particularly hot outside, or if you live somewhere that's hot all year round, you'll want to increase this amount.)

I weigh around 76 kilograms, so $76 \times 0.033 = 2.5$ litres. I should be drinking a minimum of 2.5 litres of water a day, on average. In fact, a recent European Food Safety Authority (EFSA) study suggests water intake for a non-training day should be *at least* 2.5 litres for men and 2.0 litres for women.

But remember that after exercising, in addition to replacing the water we've lost, we also need to restore our sodium levels. Sodium can be replaced through our diet. Celtic sea salt, along with being the highest quality salt that can be harvested, has a superior flavour which enhances the natural profile of most foods. It contains alkalising minerals, and is suitable for energising and replenishing electrolytes. It also helps fight bacterial infection and aids digestion.

ALCOHOL

Unfortunately, alcohol really messes with your day-to-day vitality and your ability to perform! Beer, wine and spirits are not only high in calories, but some alcohol inhibits fat oxidation, increasing unwanted body fat, which is so hard to lose the older you get. Not only that, alcohol dehydrates you (hangover, anyone?). It's what's known as a 'diuretic' and it causes your body to remove fluid from your blood through your renal system (the kidneys, bladder and ureters). It happens much quicker than you think. If you don't drink enough water along with your alcohol, you will become dehydrated very quickly.

It's also important to remember that our bodies can't digest alcohol. It passes quickly into our bloodstream and flows on to every part of our body, affecting your brain first, then your kidneys, lungs and liver. The effect depends on a variety of factors: age, lifestyle, gender and what sort of alcohol you're consuming. Undigested alcohol sits in your stomach, which is really bad for your gut health.

I don't drink much anymore. The potential setbacks to my routines and athletic goals make it a lot less exciting than it was when I was younger. On the rare occasions I do have a drink, I'll opt for a glass of good quality organic, preservative-free red wine.

Am I suggesting you completely stop drinking or socialising with your friends? Of course not. What I can say for sure is that the less alcohol you drink, the better it will be for your health, wellbeing and overall longevity. So try to moderate your drinking, or limit it to a responsible level on occasions when you're socialising or celebrating. Building alcohol-free days, weeks and even months into your routine will allow your liver and kidneys to recover and flush out the impurities. I know it's not easy, but give it a go – you won't regret it!

GUT HEALTH

Looking after your inner health comes down to two things:
LOVE YOUR LIVER and NOURISH YOUR GUT!

We must look after our liver and gut and ensure they are functioning at their best. I mentioned earlier my digestive problems when I was young that prompted me to start researching gut functionality, gut health, gut performance and gut 'mindset'. My interest in how the liver works came about partly because of my mum's health problems. I learned how a dysfunctional liver can cause so much trouble for the rest of the body, affecting everything from your dreams to your lungs.

The human gut is far more complex than we think. Three-quarters of your immune system is located within your digestive tract, and your whole immune system is protected by a fragile one-cell-thick gut lining called the 'epithelium'. If that lining is damaged or compromised, microbes and toxins can quickly spread throughout your body. When this happens, you may develop allergies to foods that you usually would have been able to digest; or you may become more fragile and more prone to getting sick. Your immune system might also become hyperactive, leading to inflammation.

As we now know, your gut is host to a vast ecosystem, filled with many organisms, collectively known as the 'microbiome'. Some five hundred million different types of bacteria live in your digestive region alone! They produce vitamins and other healing compounds, and help digest food, balance our hormones and eliminate toxins. If your microbiome is compromised, it can affect your brain function and really mess with your moods. Have you heard the expression, 'I have a gut feeling' or 'I get butterflies in my stomach when I'm nervous'? Your gut is connected to your brain through a neural cable called the vagus nerve, a long cranial nerve that runs from the brain stem through the neck and thorax and ends in the abdomen. We call it the brain–gut connection and there are some really important things to know about it:

- When anxious, some people overeat, and your body starts to produce extra feel-good chemicals, creating a vicious cycle where you believe that food and 'comfort eating' is the solution to your problems.
- Eating more adds to the feelings of stress.
- If you eat something that you have an intolerance to, gut inflammation can cause behavioural issues.
- Poor digestion can make you sluggish and less able to process information.

So, one of the most important things when trying to improve our performance, longevity and general quality of life is getting our gut health right. And that means loving your liver!

The liver plays a hugely important role in our digestion. When we eat, the gut moves all the toxic by-products from our food to our liver for processing. But toxins can quickly accumulate in the gut, liver and gallbladder if those organs are not working correctly. So, you really need to know if they're healthy. If they're not, you might experience post-meal nausea, bloating, indigestion, fatty stools, constipation, bacterial overgrowth, low thyroid activity, constant hunger and blood sugar irregularities. So remember what I said earlier:

LOVE YOUR LIVER and NOURISH YOUR GUT!

If just one of these organs or systems breaks down, the knock-on effects can be disastrous, resulting in all sorts of health problems that won't be easy to fix.

The big takeaway here is to pay attention to your digestive system and what you're eating and drinking. Make the right food choices and nourish your gut for good inner health. Most people tend to just deal with what's on the outside – lifting weights to build muscle mass and increase definition, or going on crazy, unsustainable diets to lose weight. But this can actually make you unhealthy and weaker.

A healthy gut contains a balance of good and bad bacteria. When the balance is right, you'll feel better, vital and energised – which should be no surprise since the vast majority of your body's serotonin is produced in your intestines. Remember that serotonin is the body's 'feel-good' chemical. It takes messages from the nerve cells in the brain to the rest of your body. Serotonin can elevate your mood, improve the quality and duration of your sleep, aid in the digestion of food and the expulsion of toxins, promote cellular healing, bone health and blood clotting and even increase libido.

However, if you don't have a healthy gut, your body will struggle to rid itself of toxins and you'll experience a drop in your serotonin levels. This can cause issues such as chronic fatigue and inflammation. You may also experience:

- Brain fog
- Diarrhoea
- Constipation

- Gas
- Joint pain.

So consider the brain as the 'second gut', since both organs and systems are intricately linked. If your gut isn't functioning as it should, your brain will struggle too.

Healing and maintaining good gut health takes time, commitment, focus, dedication and consistency. There is no magic pill!

Here's my checklist to ensure you have a healthy, strong gut:

- Stick to a fresh food diet.
- Eat fermented foods like kimchi, sauerkraut, yogurt or kefir (a fermented milk drink).
- Get a good night's sleep.
- Eat micronutrients – like polyphenols (fruits, vegetables, tea, dark chocolate) and foods high in fibre (seeds, whole grains).
- Hydrate, hydrate, hydrate!
- Eat slowly (chewing your food well).
- Add a good supplement to your routine that contains prebiotics and probiotics (like super greens).
- Take L-Glutamine to maintain a healthy gut lining.
- Try to lower your stress levels through activities like meditation, walking, massage, yoga, sauna etc.
- Practise 'intermittent fasting'.

Now that we've covered the reasons *why* you need a healthy gut, let's look at a few types of diet that will help you get – and keep – one!

FOUR HEALTHY GUT DIETS (PALEO, MEDITERRANEAN, PLANT-BASED AND KETO)

The paleo diet

This type of diet focuses on foods humans might have eaten during the Palaeolithic era (approximately 10,000 BC and earlier). The modern version of the paleo diet includes:

- Fruit
- Vegetables
- Lean meats
- Fish
- Eggs
- Nuts and seeds.

The idea behind this diet is that our genes have not changed sufficiently over the millennia for us to be able to properly digest all the modern foods that have evolved since farming began. Farming has provided countless benefits and allowed civilisations to grow and prosper, but farming on an industrial scale can be problematic, as the animals often feed on genetically modified grains, are frequently given hormones and other chemicals to promote growth, and many crops are artificially stimulated to promote faster growth. In addition, modern farming has made dairy products more widespread and cheaper than they've ever been. These mismatches in what we're biologically able to digest contribute to obesity, diabetes, poor gut function and heart disease in modern humans.

If you would like to learn more about the paleo diet, I highly recommend one of the best researchers in the field, Dr Chris Kresser, author of *The Paleo Cure* (www.chriskresser.com).

Generally speaking, people practising a paleo diet avoid:

- Grains (wheat, oats, barley)
- Legumes (beans, lentils, peanuts)
- Dairy products
- Added salt
- Starchy vegetables (corn, peas, white potatoes)
- Highly processed foods (chips, biscuits, TV meals etc.).

Pros of the paleo diet include:

- The elimination of white, refined carbohydrates
- The introduction of lots of vegetables
- Gets rid of processed foods
- Uses only natural sugars
- Encourages the eating of organic and free-range meat (fish, eggs, chicken)
- Potential weight loss is tied to eating the right kind of calories in the right quantity.

Cons of the paleo diet include:

- Even though it's ancient, the science behind it is still developing.
- All ultra-restrictive diets depend on discipline and tend to be hard to stick to over the long term. This can mean you quickly revert to poor dietary habits.
- Can be expensive.

Incorporating aspects of the paleo diet is just one part of my overall wellbeing regime. What's important is to find the right balance for your body. Moderation, consistency and common sense are key!

The Mediterranean diet

This diet is based on traditional cuisines from Greece, Italy, Spain, Morocco and other countries that border the Mediterranean Sea. It first became of interest to researchers in the 1950s when these populations were observed to be in better overall health, with lower rates of cardiovascular and metabolic diseases and greater longevity. The Mediterranean diet is about more than just food, though; it's a way of life.

The Mediterranean diet focuses on plant-based foods, such as whole grains, vegetables, legumes, fruits, nuts, seeds, herbs, fish, olive oil and spices. Within the Mediterranean basin, which historians call 'the cradle of civilisation', the bulk of the history of the ancient world took place. Later, during the Middle Ages, Greek and Roman diets – which incorporated bread, wine and oil products (the symbols of rural culture and agriculture), along with goat's cheese, vegetables, a little meat and lots of fish and seafood – became more and more widespread.

It's no surprise that wealthy people the world over still love fish (fried in olive oil or grilled) and seafood, especially raw or cooked oysters. In ancient times, the poor and slaves could only afford bread. They had to survive on just half a pound of olives and olive oil a month, along with some salted fish and, on the rare occasion, a little meat.

The beautiful thing about the traditional Mediterranean diet is that it offers a cuisine rich in colours, aromas and memories, giving us the taste and spirit of those who have lived in harmony with nature for a very long time. This focus on quality produce and living a balanced, holistic life is a major component when building healthy habits and increasing longevity. The Mediterranean diet proves that the combination of taste and health is a goal that everyone can pursue and build into their routine.

Key foods to eat as part of the Mediterranean diet are:

- Berries (they're high in fibre and serve as effective antioxidants)
- Nuts
- Extra-virgin olive oil
- Unsweetened Greek yogurt
- Whole grains, like quinoa
- Eggplant
- Leafy greens
- Legumes, like chickpeas (hummus).

Now you'll understand why I stick mainly to the Mediterranean diet – with elements of the paleo diet! The only change I make is to reduce the number of complex grains I eat.

The plant-based diet (vegan and vegetarian)

This diet (surprise, surprise!) focuses on foods derived primarily from plants, so fruits and vegetables, as well as nuts, seeds, oils, whole grains, beans and legumes. The plant-based diet has many restrictions – namely the exclusion of all meat and animal products. Many people now practise a 'flexitarian diet', which combines a primarily plant-based diet and its many benefits with the occasional bit of meat and other animal products. The best way to think of this approach is as a Mediterranean diet with a plant-based foundation, so it's very well balanced. Flexitarians generally don't eat meat more than a couple of times a week, though it obviously depends on individual preference.

In terms of the health benefits, a well-balanced plant-based diet can enhance our physical performance due to the high complex carbohydrate levels and high concentration of anti-oxidants and phytochemicals. However, some plant-based foods are lower in essential nutrients, like iron, zinc and protein, because they contain anti-nutritional factors like phytate (phos-phorus) and tannins. Certain nutrients can only be acquired from consuming animal products, like:

- Creatine, which increases muscular power output and enhances cognitive function
- Taurine, which may play a role in preventing heart disease
- Vitamin B12, which maintains the healthy sheaths that protect neurons in the brain
- Carnosine, which enhances antioxidant activity in the brain
- DHA, which is an omega-3 fatty acid vital for proper cognitive development and cell membrane function.

The plant-based diet has become really popular in recent years because of its health benefits and perceived positive impact on athletic performance. It's also *drastically* better for the planet, given the enormous amounts of greenhouse gases produced by meat and dairy farms and the vast swathes of land that need to be cleared for pastures. Vegetarians and vegans can consume the right amount of protein and iron if they eat legumes (eg lentils, chickpeas, beans, soy products), nuts, seeds and plant-based meat-free products. You must plan your meals well, and don't forget to take the right supplements to ensure you're not missing out on any key vitamins and minerals.

I recommend a predominantly plant-based diet, but balancing it with some meat, fish, seafood and other animal products every now and then.

Keto diet

The ketogenic diet was introduced by doctors in the 1920s as part of a treatment for epilepsy. For two decades, the therapy was used widely, but it waned with the introduction of modern drug treatments. The past 15 years have seen a re-emergence of this diet, and it continues to be the subject of much scientific interest, particularly when treating the gut microbiome, not to mention kids with epilepsy.

The keto diet is high in fats but low in carbs. Its proponents believe it's the perfect way to lose weight, enhance cognition and increase physical endurance. However, some people's bodies don't work well on a keto diet. Some have genetic problems metabolising and utilising fat. You may not benefit from being in a constant state of ketosis (when your body burns fat for energy rather than glucose). You may perform better on a low-fat diet or Mediterranean-style diet high in monounsaturated fats like olive oil.

Every time I've tried the keto diet, my body accumulated fat around my waist. I like the fasting elements of keto, and I love my 'bulletproof' coffees that blend in quality fats. When I'm on keto, I feel energetic in the morning and I'm never hungry. The Ultimate Fighting Championship (UFC) headquarters in the US recommends the keto diet to help fighters recover from brain damage after fights, as the brain needs fat. Personally, I don't avoid fat – I just don't put it on my plate as the primary food. With my frequent fasting, low intake of processed sugars and starchy foods, high plant intake, and plenty of natural wholefoods containing healthy fats (such as extra virgin olive oil), I can achieve ketosis without doing a full keto diet.

Assuming you don't have any underlying genetic issues (make sure you talk to your GP first before starting any new food regime), the keto diet might work for you. If you want to try it, remember to plan your meals well, try to eat clean and fresh food, and don't use any keto supplements. The two main issues that often arise with the keto diet are:

1. Keto focuses on animal products and avoids plant-based products, which puts you at risk of missing out on critical nutrients, such as phytochemicals, antioxidants, fibre and plant-based vitamins.

2. A high-fat, low-carb keto diet can give you symptoms known as 'keto flu', or 'carbohydrate withdrawal'. That can happen between 24 and 48 hours into a keto diet and can last from a few days to several weeks. This is simply your body shifting from glucose metabolism to fatty acid metabolism. You cut

out carbohydrates, and your insulin levels drop; this tells your kidneys to flush sodium out of your body, which can mean you lose up to 5 litres of water in just a couple of days! After this, you start to lose muscle glycogen and minerals, which can cause dizziness, nausea, headaches, muscle cramping, chills, insomnia, irritability, sugar cravings, diarrhoea and constipation. It can also mess with some people's thyroid hormones, resulting in brain fog and fatigue. And if your thyroid hormones are already low, it can raise the cortisol levels in the body. There are definitely risks in going keto!

So be careful and always talk to your physician before you start any new eating plan. You can try elements of the keto diet if you're smart with your food choices and balance your diet. There are many keto-friendly vegetables like kale, collard greens, Brussels sprouts and Swiss chard that you can mix with a small amount of low-GI fruits such as blueberries, raspberries and blackberries. This will ensure you're getting a good range of essential vitamins and minerals.

INTERMITTENT FASTING

Intermittent fasting, also known as 'intermittent energy restriction', is a broad term for various meal-timing schedules that cycle between voluntary fasting and no fasting over a given period. Remember that fasting is not about cutting calories; it's about restricting our eating time. You can still eat the same calories you usually eat in a day.

Intermittent fasting has many benefits for your body and your brain. It assists in weight loss and reduces your risk of developing type 2 diabetes, heart disease and cancer. It also boosts hormones such as HGH (human growth hormone) and testosterone.

When I fast, I do so for 15 to 16 hours max (meaning you stop fasting after 15 to 16 hours). For example, I don't eat my first meal of the day until between 10 am and noon most days. However, fasting up to 16 hours is okay every now and again, but exceeding this is not advised as it can increase your cortisol levels. Our bodies need a certain amount of cortisol in the morning to promote wakefulness and clarity as we begin focusing on the day ahead. But too much is not a good thing. Fasting in the morning is the best way to achieve a high level of focus and alertness.

Fasting also increases adrenaline (epinephrine) in the body, creating a feeling of excitement, which improves learning skills, mental focus and memory. However, high levels of adrenaline can lead to feelings of stress, panic and loss of focus or scattered thoughts.

Other benefits of intermittent fasting include:

- Improved gut microbiome
- Healthy organs
- An effective metabolism
- Liver detox (prevention of disease)
- Increased energy levels
- Blood glucose regulation
- Improved ratio of brown fats (which breaks down glucose and fat molecules)
- Weight loss (if desired).

An achievable goal might be to fast a minimum of two days and a maximum of four days per week. On other days, you can break your fast 10–12 hours after your last meal. You don't need to fast on consecutive days; you can spread the days over the week.

It's vital that you eat really well during your 'eating window'. Again, we are not cutting calories, just restricting the eating period and adding in better quality food, which will reduce your sugar cravings and bloating, and renew your energy levels.

In starting your fast:

- You will 'clean up' your food intake for two to four weeks (eliminating junk food, processed foods or foods with low nutritional value).
- In the first two weeks, you will choose two to three days to fast.
- From week three onwards, you can increase your intermediate fasting to four days if you want. Otherwise, keep it to two to three days. The main goal is long-term practice and re-education.
- After two to four weeks of clean food, you can start introducing the other foods you like in moderation, but keep fasting for three to four days per week. You can enjoy your everyday social life, but don't miss your fasting days.
- Eating organic and healthy foods during your eating window is essential. Fasting won't work if you consume lots of processed foods or excessive calories. (Remember, we are not cutting calories; we are eating better quality food.)

What you should *avoid* eating for two to four weeks

- High carbohydrate and processed foods (pizza, bread, pasta, white potato)
- Dairy products (cow's milk, cheese, yogurt)
- Grains and cereals (oats, couscous, corn, buckwheat)
- Soft drinks, including sports drinks
- Low-carb and meal replacement bars
- Alcohol
- Lollies
- Milk chocolate
- Cakes, including pastries and biscuits
- Sauces.

What you can *enjoy* eating during this time

- Veggies (dark greens are best) such as broccoli, zucchini, Brussels sprouts, asparagus
- Salads (all leaves)
- Carrots, sweet potato, beetroot, yams, tomatoes, cauliflower
- Brown rice or quinoa
- Olives (which are high in fats and protein)
- Cabbage
- Onion, chilli
- Green juices and smoothies
- Fruits (pears, apples, red papaya, bananas, blueberries, strawberries, blackberries, pineapple)
- Dark chocolate (85 per cent cocoa or above)
- Eggs
- Kimchi, sauerkraut, kefir, kombucha – fermented foods are

essential to help build the gut flora. (If you are looking to cut out sugar, opt for kefir over kombucha.)

MEAT (ORGANIC, GRASS-FED OR SUSTAINABLY FARMED)

Try to eat meat during the day, and salmon, white fish, chicken and prawns at night. Choose lighter meals for dinner, which are easier to digest and lead to deeper sleep.

- Beef, lamb
- Pork (high quality)
- Poultry such as chicken, duck, turkey
- Seafood such as prawns and fish.

FATS/OILS (OKAY WHILE COOKING)
- Organic butter (if you are okay with dairy)
- Ghee
- Coconut oil
- Olive oil.

SALTS
- Himalayan salt
- Celtic sea salt.

DRINKS

You can drink water, coffee and tea during the fasting period, which will help reduce hunger pangs.

NUTS/FATS (OKAY WHILE COOKING)
- Almonds

- Macadamias
- Hazelnuts
- Brazil nuts
- Cashews
- Avocado.

WHAT YOUR AVERAGE DAY WILL LOOK LIKE

- An early-evening dinner is the best and easiest way to start intermittent fasting.
- Finish dinner by 7 pm, and break your fast at 11 am the following day.
- Finish dinner at 6 pm, and break your fast at 10 am the following day. (I try to have my dinner at 5 pm or 6 pm at the latest.)
- If you eat anything after dinner, you will break your fast and need to restart the process. But you won't break your fast if you eat something low in glucose or with a maximum of 50 calories. The key is not to eat anything with more than 50 calories (so no chocolate).
- Walking after dinner helps your digestion and quickly gets you into your fasting state, but the walking must be light – anything prolonged or strenuous can spike your insulin levels and break the fast.

What are you allowed to eat *during* your fast?
- Black coffee
- Six strawberries or half a pear

- Ginger or peppermint tea
- Lemon with water
- Anything under 50 calories that's low in glucose and insulin (e.g. miso soup, teaspoon of peanut butter, five cashews, 40 g of yoghurt, bite of a banana).

While you are fasting, ensure that you
- Drink plenty of water, as the body can get dehydrated during fasting. (Drinking water will also help you detox and reduce your appetite.)
- Increase salt intake (I like Celtic sea salt), or use electrolyte powders.

What to eat when you break your fast for better digestion and breakdown of fats
- Bone broth
- Green juice
- Probiotic drink
- Green smoothie (with super green supplement).

And straightaway you can have your first meal. Make it lunch and make it the biggest meal of the day, then eat lightly for the rest of the day.

MY GO-TO DAILY ROUTINE

First thing (5 am):
- One cup of purified water (300 ml)

- Half a cup of warm water with half a lemon or lime squeezed into it (helps to reduce hunger)
- Two teaspoons or one scoop of super greens (a maximum of 35 to 50 calories so you aren't breaking your fast)
- Five tablets of aminos if you have a good one that does not break your fasting
- Take all these supplements before having coffee and going to work.

Mid-morning:
- Break your fast after 16 hours: drink 1 cup of bone broth before having breakfast or lunch (remember, no bread). Or you can have a green smoothie if you prefer.
- If you have breakfast, go for it! Take three probiotics with breakfast – the same with lunch. Eat well!
- If you feel low in energy before exercising, have a black coffee with five aminos (particularly if you are fasting).

Lunchtime:
- The most significant meal of the day (especially if you didn't have breakfast), so make it bigger.

Afternoon tea:
- Eat a healthy snack. Otherwise, you can have all your calories between lunch and dinner.
- Smoothie or eat some light protein.
- You can have a big meal if you prefer. (Remember, you want your calories.)

Dinner:

- Light dinner (2 to 3 hours before bed)
- White meat is best
- It's okay to have dinner out or a bigger meal here if it's a social occasion
- Vegetarian dinners work well at this time of day
- L-glutamine: 5 grams before bed
- Magnesium: 400 milligrams before bed.

Important reminder: if you need to eat four meals during the eating window, don't extend the window to fit them in. You shouldn't limit yourself to one or two meals. You need calories to fuel your body, perform well and be happy.

THE MORNING ROUTINE: SEVEN PILLARS FOR A BETTER LIFE

1. Know when you need to wake up so your routine isn't rushed. As you rise, make sure you have a big smile on your face to greet the new day and show gratitude.

2. Scrape your tongue to remove all the lingering bacteria. This is an Ayurvedic practice that improves digestion and gut health.

3. Drink 500 ml of purified water to wake up the digestion and brain. Hydration first thing in the morning is essential.

4. Ten to 20 minutes of meditation followed by breathwork (see Chapters 5 and 6).

5. Move your body for 10 to 30 minutes (a mix of mobility, stretching and cardio work).

6. If fasting, don't eat anything until 9 am, 10 am or noon, depending on when you had your last meal and went to bed.

7. Exercise for at least an hour, preferably in the morning so the day doesn't get away from you.

SMOOTHIE RECIPES

Blitzing healthy ingredients together to make a delicious fresh smoothie each morning is a tasty and nutritious way to start your day. Smoothies can be a versatile, portable post-workout snack, too, and they couldn't be easier to prepare — all you need is to add the ingredients to a blender and process to your desired consistency. Whey is a great protein powder substitute if you're avoiding dairy, as it contains beneficial nutrients.

Mango Efficiency

An ideal breakfast or lunch, or to help you refuel after training.

flesh of ½ mango, roughly chopped

30 g vegan protein powder (vanilla or natural flavour)

1 teaspoon almond butter

1 teaspoon omega-3 fish oil

½ cup coconut water

½ cup filtered tap water

The Strawberries Effect

I like to think of this as a big meal in a glass. It's a good one to break the fast, as a filling lunch or post training. I prefer the texture of frozen strawberries, but use whatever is available.

8 strawberries

30 g vegan protein powder (vanilla or natural flavour)

¼–½ avocado

½ cup coconut kefir

½ cup filtered tap water

Banana Boost

I can make this fortifying smoothie in less than a minute, any time of the day.

1½ frozen bananas

100 g sugar-free organic raw açaí

30 g vegan protein powder (vanilla or natural flavour)

1 teaspoon cashew butter

1 cup filtered tap water

The Popeye Papaya

Fermented foods are essential to help build gut flora, hence the inclusion of kefir in this smoothie. Colostrum may be good for immunity and gut health.

flesh of ¼ papaya, roughly chopped

1 cup goat's milk kefir

30 g vegan protein powder (vanilla or natural flavour)

1 teaspoon colostrum powder

Green smoothie to break your fast

Glutamine is the most abundant amino acid (building block of protein) in the body. It can make enough for its regular needs, but during times of extreme stress (such as after heavy exercise), it may need more glutamine than it can make.

250 ml coconut water

1 scoop super greens powder

5 g L-glutamine

¼ avocado

1 kiwi fruit

Green smoothie for a snack or meal

Spirulina is a concentrated source of vitamins and minerals, and so practical in its powdered form.

1 handful spinach

¼ avocado

30 g vegan protein powder (vanilla or natural flavour)

1 teaspoon spirulina

200 ml filtered water or coconut water

Mixed Berry Bowl

You might need to use a spatula to scrape down the sides of your blender and make sure everything is thoroughly mixed as this is thicker than a regular smoothie – hence serving it in a bowl with a spoon.

2 cups mixed frozen berries

150 ml coconut milk

30 g vegan protein powder (vanilla or natural flavour)

BREAKFAST RECIPES

Eating a nutritious breakfast is one of the pillars of establishing the kind of morning routine that will help to achieve your main goal: optimum health and the best chances for longevity.

The Boiled Eggs Break

Eggs are a convenient and versatile lean protein source that are more affordable than other options. They are also one of the few foods that naturally contain Vitamin D, which is needed for strong bones, muscles and overall health.

4 eggs

½ avocado

10 ml olive oil

50 g Greek-style feta, cubed

pinch of Celtic sea salt

½ red papaya

1 banana

Place eggs in a saucepan and fill with enough cold water to cover them by about 3 cm. Bring to the boil and cook for 8–10 minutes, then strain and run cold water over the eggs for 2 minutes.

Shell and slice the eggs.

Cube the avocado flesh, mix with the eggs and drizzle with the olive oil.

Scatter over the feta and a pinch of Celtic sea salt.

Serve with slices of papaya and banana.

The Scramble Effect

I don't scramble my eggs with any dairy in the pan, preferring pure eggs with a pinch of garlic salt. (You can easily make your own by combining 3 parts salt with 1 part dried or fresh, finely chopped garlic. Regular Celtic sea salt is also good.) It's very hard for me to eat bread, but when I do, I'm very picky and go for gluten-free.

3 eggs
pinch of garlic salt
2 slices bread
1 teaspoon ghee
½ avocado
100 g blueberries, to serve

Heat a small non-stick frying pan over a medium heat, then crack the eggs into it, add a pinch of garlic salt and cook for approx. 1 minute, stirring frequently.

Toast the bread, spread with the ghee then smash avocado on top and spoon over the eggs.

Serve with blueberries.

Shredded Chicken with Smashed Avocado and Fruit

I can't think of a heartier way to start the day that's ready so quickly.

Smash half an avocado with a drizzle of olive oil and a pinch of Celtic sea salt, and sprinkle with a handful of fresh, roughly chopped coriander leaves. Serve with 125 g shredded roast chicken.

In a separate bowl, stir together the chopped flesh of half a red papaya and half a mango with 150 g coconut yogurt and a teaspoon of honey.

Açaí Bowl

Bright purple açaí berries come from a palm tree native to the Amazon rainforest in my beloved Brazil.

2 frozen bananas

150 ml coconut milk

30 g vegan protein powder (vanilla or natural flavour)

300 g organic raw açaí

1 tablespoon almond butter

Put the bananas and coconut milk in a blender and process to a thick cream consistency. Add the protein powder and mix well. Break the açaí into small pieces and add to the blender. Mix, stopping a couple of times to scrape down the sides with a spoon, until the smoothie's the consistency of a thick paste. Pour into a bowl, topping with almond butter to finish.

LUNCH RECIPES

Eating a varied, well-balanced diet means eating a mixture of foods that will provide you with different types and amounts of key nutrients. It can be tempting to eat just the foods we like, that are familiar or we find easy to prepare, but cooking a range of dishes will help make your meals more interesting, so that you don't grow bored of your diet.

Slow Cooker (4–6 hour) Brisket just with salt, garlic and olive oil

My plate contains 135 g brisket, 200 g baked sweet potato, 100 g steamed broccoli and a quarter of an avocado. You might not be used to weighing portions of your meal, but as people tend to eat almost all of whatever they serve themselves, it's a quick and effective way to prevent overindulgence.

1–1½ tablespoons Celtic sea salt
6–8 garlic cloves, peeled and finely chopped
2 tablespoons olive oil
1.5–1.75 kg beef brisket

Preheat the oven to 160°C fan-forced/180°C conventional.

Combine the salt and garlic in a bowl, then stir in the olive oil.

Place the brisket in a deep-sided roasting tin, then rub the garlic and salt mixture all over.

Cover with foil and leave to marinate for 20 minutes. Place in the oven and cook for 4–6 hours until the meat is tender.

At the 3-hour-point, you can remove the foil so the top can crisp up.

When cooked, remove from the oven and allow to rest before slicing.

SWEET POTATO

I keep the skin on my sweet potato, so simply scrub it and cut into 5 cm pieces, place in an ovenproof dish in a single layer and drizzle with 1 tablespoon olive oil and sprinkle over a pinch of Celtic sea salt. Bake on the top shelf of the oven for approx. 45 minutes.

BROCCOLI

I steam broccoli florets until just tender with 1 teaspoon of ghee and a sprinkling of Celtic sea salt.

Moroccan-style Oven-baked Chicken Thighs

My plate contains 125 g baked chicken thigh meat, 100 g baked broccolini, half an avocado, 20 g of sauerkraut or kimchi, and then 1 kiwi fruit and 1 pear for dessert.

6 small or 8 large chicken thighs, skin on

1 tablespoon olive oil

1 tablespoon Moroccan seasoning

Preheat the oven to 100°C fan-forced/120°C conventional.

Place the chicken into a large bowl, add the olive oil then sprinkle over the Moroccan seasoning. I use my hands to rub the spices into the meat, but you can also stir everything together with a large spoon to coat.

Leave to marinade for 10–20 minutes.

Transfer to an ovenproof roasting dish, cover with foil and bake for 2 hours or until the chicken is cooked through. You can remove the foil for the last 20 minutes to allow the meat to crisp up, and use a meat thermometer to check the internal temperature is at 74°C.

BROCCOLI

Cut a head of broccoli into small florets.

Line a baking tray with baking paper and place the broccoli on top.

Drizzle with olive oil and sprinkle with a pinch of Celtic sea salt.

Bake on the top shelf of the oven for approx. 45–60 minutes, checking after 30 minutes to make sure it doesn't burn.

Turkey Mince Cooked with Spices, Grated Zucchini and Herbs

My plate contains 135 g turkey mince with 50 g zucchini, 60 g quinoa and half an avocado, plus the flesh of 1 mango.

¼ onion (about 45 g), peeled and finely chopped

4 garlic cloves, peeled and finely chopped

¼ bunch coriander, leaves and stems finely chopped

2 teaspoons chilli flakes

juice of ¼ lime

1 teaspoon Celtic sea salt

2 teaspoons olive oil

500 g turkey mince

½ tablespoon ghee

1 medium-size zucchini, grated

Place the first 7 ingredients in a food processor and process to a thick paste, or use a mortar and pestle.

In a large bowl, combine the mince and spice mix — I like to use my hands to thoroughly work the flavour into the meat.

Heat the ghee in a frying pan over a medium heat and cook the mince for 8–10 minutes, stirring often.

Scatter over the zucchini, stir to combine and cover with a lid. Cook for a further 3–4 minutes.

QUINOA

Rinse 1 cup of quinoa in a sieve under running water.

Melt 2 teaspoons ghee in a saucepan over a medium heat and fry 2 finely chopped garlic cloves for 2 minutes.

Add the rinsed quinoa and stir to coat in the ghee.

Add 2 cups boiling water and simmer gently until the quinoa has absorbed all the water and is tender, approx. 15 minutes.

DINNER RECIPES

I love light dinners because they are easy to digest, which helps me enjoy a more restful night's sleep and aids effective recovery. I always look to lean protein in the evening, which sits better in my digestive system. I also leave my quality carbs for dinner; they help switch on my parasympathetic nervous system by promoting serotonin release and reducing cortisol levels.

Grilled Red Snapper with Lime, Garlic, Olive Oil and Pink Himalayan Salt

My plate contains 150 g grilled red snapper (I tend to go for skin-on fillets, for the beneficial omega-3 fats they contain), 100 g steamed broccoli, 100 g steamed carrots, 100 g steamed sweet potato, 15 ml olive oil drizzled over the veggies, 1 tablespoon kimchi and 150 g mango for dessert.

4 garlic cloves, peeled and finely chopped

½ teaspoon pink Himalayan salt

1 tablespoon olive oil

juice of ½ lime

150 g red snapper fillet

steamed vegetables, kimchi, to serve

Combine the garlic, salt, olive oil and lime juice in a bowl, then add the fish and gently turn to coat in the mixture.

Cover and leave to marinate for 10–15 minutes.

Preheat the grill to medium. Transfer the snapper fillet to a heatproof tray and grill for approx. 10 minutes, turning halfway.

Serve with steamed broccoli, carrots and sweet potato drizzled with olive oil and seasoned with a pinch of garlic salt, a tablespoon of kimchi and 150 g mango for dessert.

Grilled Chicken Breast with Mixed Herbs

I like to use herbed sea salt in this dish (Herbamare is my favourite), but you can substitute a store-bought herbal seasoning with mixed dried herbs and Celtic sea salt.

My plate contains 125 g grilled skinless chicken breast, a handful of mixed salad leaves drizzled with 15 ml olive oil and seasoned with a pinch of Himalayan salt, 40 g brown rice or quinoa, ½ avocado, 6 green olives and 20 g sauerkraut.

1 chicken breast

½ teaspoon herb-infused salt, or ¼ teaspoon Celtic sea salt and
   ¼ teaspoon mixed dried herbs

Place the chicken breast in a bowl and rub with salt and herbs. Cover and leave for 10 minutes.

Preheat the grill to medium and transfer the chicken to a heatproof tray. Cook for approx. 7–8 minutes each side until cooked through.

BROWN RICE

Rinse 1 cup brown rice under running water. Fry in 1 tablespoon ghee with 3 peeled and chopped garlic cloves over a medium heat for 3 minutes, stirring constantly, then add 2 cups water and a pinch of salt. Cover, bring to the boil and simmer gently for 25–35 minutes until all the water has been absorbed.

Mixed Salad

Homemade hummus is very easy to make and it tastes much better than store-bought. Drain and tip a tin of chickpeas into a food processor. Peel and add a small clove of garlic, a good squeeze of lemon juice, 1 tablespoon olive oil and a pinch of salt, then blitz until smooth.

15 ml olive oil

juice of ¼ lime

pinch of pink Himalayan salt

100 g carrots

100 g zucchini

2 garlic cloves

1 tablespoon ghee

½ avocado, cubed

1 handful mixed salad leaves

goat's cheese

15 g sauerkraut

1 hard-boiled egg, chopped

1 tablespoon hummus

Mix the olive oil, lime juice and salt in a small bowl and set aside.

Thinly slice the carrots and zucchini, steam them for two minutes until just tender, transfer to a frying pan with the garlic and ghee and cook for another two minutes over a medium heat. Remove from the heat and leave to cool.

To assemble, stir the avocado into the salad leaves and pour over the dressing then pile into the middle of a plate. Around it arrange the carrots and zucchini, with goat's cheese, sauerkraut, egg and hummus. I often finish this dinner with 100 g of strawberries.

Japanese-style Tofu with Bok Choy and Quinoa

250 g firm tofu

4 garlic cloves

small thumb fresh ginger

1 tablespoon soy sauce

1–2 bunches bok choy

4 tablespoons ghee

50 g cooked quinoa and 1 tablespoon kimchi, to serve

Cut the tofu into 2 cm cubes and place in a bowl.

Peel and finely chop the garlic, and peel and mince the ginger. Add to the bowl.

Pour over the soy sauce and stir gently, then cover and leave to marinate in the fridge for at least 30 minutes (overnight is best).

Separate the bok choy leaves and stems and rinse thoroughly under running water.

Heat 2 tablespoons of the ghee in a wok or large frying pan over a high heat. Stir-fry the bok choy for 2–3 minutes. We want it to be crunchy and not steamed.

Remove from the pan and set aside.

Add the remaining 2 tablespoons of ghee to the pan and stir-fry the tofu for 2 minutes.

To assemble, place some bok choy in the middle of a plate, spoon over the quinoa then the tofu, and serve with the kimchi on the side.

SNACKS

Snacks can be part of your daily nutrition, and keeping healthy options on hand is a powerful way to incorporate consistency into your pursuit of longevity. It's important to make sensible choices and watch your portion size. I will eat a protein bar or have a protein shake as a last resort, but my preference is to consume a combination of protein, fats and carbohydrates for each snack – and for them to come from unprocessed sources.

Bone Broth

When I have time, I love to make my own bone broth, but when life gets busy, using a paste from a jar of concentrate (GevityRx and Best of the Bone are my favourites) is such a convenient way to consume gelatin, collagen, vitamins and minerals – you simply dissolve 1 teaspoon in a mug of hot water. Check out my bone broth recipe on YouTube.

Green Smoothie

It's never a bad thing to have a vegan option in your repertoire. The avocado makes this nutrient-dense smoothie deliciously creamy.

2 handfuls kale or rainbow chard, stems removed

½ avocado

juice of ½ lime

large handful frozen pineapple chunks

small thumb fresh ginger, peeled

1 tablespoon cashew nuts

1 banana

My Favourite Fruit Snack

Simply mix together 200 g mixed berries and 100–150 g coconut yogurt, and top with 1 teaspoon almond butter.

Papaya Performance

Remove the seeds from half a red papaya then serve with 1 tablespoon unsalted cashew nuts.

Shredded Chicken

This has to be the quickest snack plate in the world.

80–100 g shredded roast chicken

1 pear, cored and sliced

1 kiwi fruit

Creamy Blueberries

Combine 150 g blueberries with 1 cup (250 g) Greek yoghurt or goat's kefir (coconut kefir is a good vegan alternative) and 1 tablespoon unsalted cashew nuts.

5.
ENERGISE AND REFRESH – THE IMPORTANCE OF BREATHING

Most of us take breathing for granted – we do it all day long and it happens automatically, so why should we pay much attention to it? Well, breathing is fundamental for our physical and mental health and concentrating on exactly *how* we breathe has a big effect on our energy levels and general wellbeing.

'Breathwork' is a powerful tool that helps us stay connected and allows us to tap into our inner strength. We become more resilient in the calming space we create. By breathing deeply and consciously, we improve our longevity and boost our immunity.

We can survive without food for weeks, and a few days without water, but deprived of air we'd be gone in minutes. When we think about our health, we spend a lot of time and attention on what we eat and drink, but rarely do we give the same consideration to the air we breathe (until it's polluted) and the volume of air we need to put through our respiratory system. How crazy is that? Examining the quality and quantity of the air we breathe is essential in understanding the relationship between oxygen and the body.

Breathwork has been practised in cultures around the world for thousands of years. Thankfully Western science has caught up and now realises how important it is. But breathing correctly it isn't as easy as you'd think. Our environment has dramatically changed over the centuries, with modified foods, poor nutrition, chronic stress, a sedentary lifestyle, overheated homes and a general lack of fitness and awareness of the body all contributing to poor breathing. Modern society places a greater emphasis on 'health and lifestyle', but at the same time so much of modern life works *against* holistic health. We are facing more and more health problems, from poor posture and chronic back complaints to delayed development from birth to teenagers. We've created these problems. Then we spend huge amounts of time and money trying to correct them! The irony is that it doesn't cost anything to breathe correctly, and it doesn't take too much of your time to learn and practise a few simple breathwork exercises.

At its most basic level, breathing provides oxygen for metabolism – the cellular process that burns food to generate energy – and removes the by-product of these chemical reactions, carbon dioxide. Carbon dioxide is associated with lactic acid accumulation and too much of it in the bloodstream can result in metabolic issues and cell damage. Breathing is also one of our most important 'PH regulators', balancing the levels of 'acids' and 'bases' in the body. Breathing affects the autonomic nervous system (the functions we don't have to think about, like heart rate and digestion), as well as our circulation. Our body's systems should function as nature intended, before our modern lifestyle got in the way, and breathing is one of the key mechanisms to ensure that happens.

Conscious breathing sends messages to the brain to calm us down, decreasing the body's stress responses. It retrains the nervous system's automatic response to environmental triggers and allows us to calmly back away from danger, or to deal with the threat with a positive mindset. We tend to use our *sympathetic* nervous system too much – our 'fight or flight' response that stimulates the production of adrenaline and noradrenaline – increasing our heart rate and blood pressure. We lose control of our breathing and our stress levels go through the roof. Through breathwork, we can manage that response and switch on our *parasympathetic* nervous system, which quiets our body and mind and conserves our energy, restoring us to a calm and composed state.

To deal with my asthma attacks and bronchitis when I was younger, I had to learn to improve and open up the airways in my lungs. I'd sit down and try to control the tempo and depth of my breathing to calm my mind and steady my heart rate – a big inhalation, then a long slow exhalation. Once I'd recovered, I could keep doing whatever I was doing – mainly swimming and conditioning exercises. It was tough as a kid when your mind is racing and you want to keep playing. But I was forced to adapt and learn because I was getting really sick, and focusing on my breathing and the role of my diaphragm was a way of regulating my nervous system and, consequently, my health. After four years in the program, my respiratory problems were gone. I can't actually remember when I last had an asthma attack or was breathless!

The benefits of breath exercises include:

- Pain relief
- Stress management (switch on the parasympathetic nervous system to calm ourselves)
- Improved immune system (high stress levels compromise immunity)
- Improved digestive system and gut health
- Improved sleep patterns
- Supports correct posture
- Builds energy levels and improves endurance
- Lowers blood pressure
- Stimulates the lymphatic system (helps to detox the body)
- There are even studies that suggest breathing exercises may be linked to weight loss and a reduction in body fat.

Later in my life, after years on the road, I returned to Australia and began to study the methods of holistic health and personal development with expert Paul Chek. At the time, Paul was introducing breathwork into his training and rehabilitation methods. Paul teaches his clients how to 'switch on' the diaphragm, breathe through the nose and maintain core activation to protect the spine and improve the posture.

Later still, I got to spend a week with another legend, Wim Hof, and learn about his breathing methods and how they applied to his ground-breaking exploration of the benefits of ice baths. Wim Hof's technique increases the amount of oxygen the body can absorb and decreases the absorption of carbon dioxide, which induces hyperventilation.

Another big step in my education came when I had the opportunity to learn 'Surf Apnoea' training, a technique used by a lot of surfers, ocean swimmers and free-divers – any type of water athlete, really. The technique teaches you how to hold your breath to help manage your carbon dioxide tolerance. This helps you handle stress, particularly during high-stakes situations, like being held under water in heavy surf conditions.

But my most significant step with breathwork came through yoga, where one of the main aims is to connect different poses through 'flow', affecting the sympathetic and parasympathetic nervous systems. Breath practice in yoga is called *pranayama*. *Prana* means 'breath' or 'life force', and *ayama* means 'expansion' or 'control'. The concept aims to use the breath – your life force – to expand your consciousness and calm your mind. The physical poses in yoga help us to focus on our breath. The movements are controlled and connected through each breath's timing and the duration of the inhalation and exhalation. Holding the positions produces internal heat and raises our levels of carbon dioxide tolerance. The goals are to connect your body and mind, supply oxygen through all the systems of the body and simultaneously expel toxins and stress.

The benefits of *pranayama* breathwork include:

- Decreases stress
- Improves sleep quality
- Improves lung capacity
- Enhances cognitive performance
- Develops mindfulness
- Lowers blood pressure

- Improves metabolism and energy creation
- Enhances brain function.

Science, academic research and the weight of human experience testify to the benefits of yoga breathing techniques. These techniques have profound effects on our mental awareness and cognition, the connection between the body and the mind, our respiratory health, biochemical processes and metabolic functions. Under the safe guidance of a coach, specialist or yoga teacher, yoga breathing techniques have also been found to be useful in managing a range of clinical conditions.

Now that we have a basic understanding of the benefits of breathwork, let's get started!

DIAPHRAGMATIC BREATHING

Did you know that the *way* we breathe fundamentally affects our health, strength and longevity? Many of us tend to take shallow breaths, which isn't good. 'Diaphragmatic breathing', on the other hand, also known as 'belly breathing' or 'deep breathing', is a powerful technique that trains and strengthens our respiratory system.

The diaphragm is the primary breathing muscle in your body, dividing the chest from the abdomen. It contracts when you inhale, pulling the lungs down, stretching and expanding the rib cage, and then relaxes back into a 'dome' position when you exhale, reducing the air in the lungs.

Breathing from the diaphragm is the difference between

shallow pants – which is common when we're in stressful situations or in 'fight or flight' mode – and the slow, deep inhalations through the nose that open up the chest, rib cage and lungs more fully. Have you ever been told that you should breathe through your belly on your first inhalation, and that the oxygen should go straight through the belly? Do you remember your confusion? A lot of people don't understand the technique or that it's even possible. The belly is where we digest food, so it's easy to forget it's also integral to how we breathe. In this section, I'll explain the easy way to breathe using your diaphragm and how important it is to work on it every single day.

HOW TO PRACTISE DIAPHRAGMATIC BREATHING

1. Lie down in a comfortable place. Bend your knees and close your eyes. Place a pillow under your head or neck if it helps you feel more relaxed.

2. Place one hand on your belly and one hand on your rib cage. The hand on your belly is to feel the movement, and the one on your rib cage is to feel the expansion towards the chest after your belly is full.

3. Inhale through your nose for four to six seconds, feeling your belly expand. You may feel a slight tight tension or restriction the first few times.

4. Hold your breath for three seconds.

5. Exhale very slowly and steadily through your nose. You should feel your chest and rib cage dropping first and your belly after. Remember to inhale through your belly; the rib cage and chest will fill up first. Keep this sequence in your mind.

6. Repeat this for 5 to 10 minutes or through 10 to 30 breaths.

A couple of tips:

- If you're having trouble breathing in this position, get closer to the wall, put your feet flat against it and keep your knees bent – you can even use a chair, couch or a Swiss ball to raise your legs. This posture works with the body's anatomy, which is helpful for those who have trouble switching on their diaphragm.
- Don't worry if you can't breathe through your diaphragm on the first attempt. Keep trying; it will happen! Just like anything else involving the body's movements, it's a skill that requires practice, and with practice it gets easier. Eventually, you'll be able to do it in all different kinds of positions – even while moving through a series of yoga poses.

Once you learn the basics, you can train by activating your diaphragm while crawling, sitting, walking, squatting, dead-lifting or driving.

The most efficient way to breathe

In addition to acting as the primary respiratory muscle, the diaphragm also contributes to vocalisation and swallowing. When the diaphragm is not functioning as it should, various disorders can arise, including respiratory illnesses, poor posture, poor sleep patterns, exercise intolerance and even more life-threatening conditions.

Research shows that mind–body exercises like tai chi and yoga that use diaphragmatic breathing can reduce stress in individuals in high-pressure situations, or who are overwhelmed with negative emotions, by modulating the 'sympathetic–vagal balance'. The sympathetic–vagal balance toggles us between using our sympathetic nervous system ('fight or flight') and the parasympathetic nervous system (calm and control). The vagus nerve, as we discussed earlier, runs from your brain to your gut and carries important signals back and forth. Diaphragmatic breathing stimulates the vagus nerve, keeping us calm, rested, and in a good mood with a moderate heart rate.

The benefits of diaphragmatic breathing include

- Helps you relax, decreasing stress
- Increases oxygen levels in your blood
- Reduces blood pressure
- Improves muscle function during exercises and prevents injuries
- Helps to strengthen your core
- Improves posture and spine stability
- Helps to decompress the spine
- Boosts the immune system

- Improves digestion
- Relieves pain
- Builds up energy and motivation
- Decreases muscle tension
- Makes breathing more efficient, conserving energy
- May increase antioxidant activity and reduce oxidative stress in the body after exercise in athletes.

How often should I practise diaphragmatic breathing?

Five to 10 minutes, four to five days a week should be enough! Just add it to your routine that we set up earlier. I motivate the athletes I coach to incorporate a breathing routine as part of their pre-event warm-up – 10 to 30 breaths on full inhale and complete exhale, in through the nose, out through the nose. Remember that the mouth is meant for eating, and the nose is meant for breathing! (I will explain more about that shortly.) I practise diaphragmatic breathing every day before I start my meditation, on my warm-ups before weight training, and when I'm getting into any basic movement pattern.

NASAL BREATHING

Most of us breathe through our mouths, especially when we're exercising or exerting ourselves. However, *nasal* breathing (through our nose) has been shown to greatly benefit longevity. It's the natural way our bodies are designed to breathe. When we breathe through our noses, our airways are humidified, filtered and warmed, which helps to improve lung capacity and prevent infections. You are less likely to get sick or suffer from respiratory issues. Maintaining a consistent exercise routine is easier. Nasal breathing also increases the amount of oxygen delivered to your body, boosting endurance and athletic performance.

When we breathe through our mouths, the air goes straight to our lungs, bypassing the nasal passage specifically designed to help oxygenate the body. Nasal breathing helps to strengthen the diaphragm, improving our posture and core stability. This allows you to move more easily – with more flow and confidence – improving your overall strength. Nasal breathing can also help improve the quality of our sleep by keeping our airways open. When we breathe through our mouth while sleeping, the airways can become obstructed, leading to snoring and sleep apnoea. So, if you want to sleep better and feel refreshed in the morning, consider adding some nasal breathing exercises to your bedtime routine.

Most people don't care much about the nose, unless we're talking about its look and shape! It's funny but true. People don't understand – or have never been told – how beneficial it is to breathe through the nose. They try to change the nose's shape to whatever look is in fashion, often thinking the nose should be broad and open. But the nose is the narrowest part of the respiratory tract – like a bottleneck – and the airflow is most constricted as it enters the lungs. We breathe around 20,000 times a day through our nose, so we can appreciate the extra work involved when we learn that it filters out allergens, bacteria and viruses. The American fitness guru Ben Greenfield notes in his book, *Boundless*, that our nose hairs are estimated to protect our body from about 20 billion particles of foreign matter *daily*.

So go the nose!

BREATHE SAFELY, EFFICIENTLY AND PROPERLY

Nasal breathing is a simple yet effective practice that anyone can incorporate into their daily routine. Start with a short session and gradually increase as your body becomes comfortable with the practice.

Here are a few simple nasal breathing exercises that you can try.

Alternate nostril breathing

Alternate nostril breathing is a type of *pranayama* in yoga, also known as *nadi shodhana*. *Nadi* is a Sanskrit word meaning 'channel', and *shodhana* means 'cleansing' or 'purifying'. This type of breathwork doesn't just belong to the yoga tradition, however. It's often used in mindfulness and relaxation practice to help calm the body and the mind.

I remember when I first learned how to do alternate nostril breathing. I was only seventeen years old, and I was practising a lot of Brazilian capoeira – an acrobatic combination of martial arts and dance. I also started practising Hatha yoga, which balances the mind and the body through a combination of poses and breathing exercises. I was reading lots of books about the life of the samurai and ancient routines from Japanese and Indian culture. An emphasis on the breath was a common thread running through all of these disciplines, and one I delved into and quickly built into my health regime.

The technique is simple: you inhale through one nostril by using your finger to close the other nostril, then repeat the process the other way. It takes a bit of practice, so it is an excellent mindfulness exercise as well. The aim is to control your breath through focus and attention, which is a good step towards a deeper breath that connects the mind and body.

HOW TO ALTERNATE NOSTRIL BREATHE

1. Find a quiet place to sit, without distractions.

2. Bring your right hand up to your face ❶. Place your thumb on your right nostril and press to close it.

3. With the nostril covered, close your eyes and exhale thoroughly and slowly through your left nostril ❷.

4. Once you fully exhale, release your right nostril, and put your ring finger on your left nostril.

5. Inhale deeply and slowly from the right side. Make sure your breath is smooth and continuous.

6. Once you have inhaled completely, close the right nostril in the same manner as in step 2 and exhale through your left nostril.

7. When you finish the exhalation through the left nostril, you will start to inhale slowly through the left nostril. When it's complete, close the left nostril in the same manner as in step 4 and slowly exhale through the right nostril.

8. Repeat the technique for 5–10 minutes or 10–20 reps. You can do alternate nostril breathing for as short or long a period as you like.

Alternate breathing can also help ground you before meditation. Sometimes it takes a lot of work to settle into meditation – the brain can be racing, distracted by the day's problems. If you complete a few rounds of this focused breathing technique, it will help settle you into your session.

Taping your mouth

This breathwork technique is fascinating *and* challenging. Why? Every time I ask one of my students to try it, they look confused and alarmed. 'Do *what*? I'm going to die! Are you crazy? No way! For what?'

But there's really nothing to worry about. You won't die! Taping the mouth can improve athletic performance and sleep patterns, and help with recovery. You can use the technique during your exercises and when you are sleeping. As I've mentioned, a lot of people sleep with their mouths open, which can lead to snoring, a dry mouth and oral hygiene problems. Breathing through your nose will help you sleep better and increase your oxygen intake. The air will be filtered, clean and warm, which will help your immunity and improve physical performance.

It can take four to eight weeks of mouth tape training before you'll be able to breathe through your nose without the use of tape. But an important note before starting: don't use duct tape or anything that isn't really gentle and porous! Check the tape quality, otherwise you'll likely experience skin irritation, an allergic reaction, or a rash. Talk to your doctor or find a tape that sits well on your skin and can be removed easily. The two types of tape I recommend are MyoTape and 3M Transpore Surgical Tape. But before applying either, make sure you lightly moisturise your lips and the skin around your mouth.

I suggest starting slowly, maybe at home during the day or after dinner but before bed. Begin by taping your mouth for an hour or two, then gradually increase the time increments, and, when you are feeling comfortable, try it while you sleep.

For performance training, start by taping your mouth during select exercises, like when you're working your lower body or upper body sets. While resting, take the tape off, reset, and reapply it when you perform another set of reps. Performance athletes can increase the length of time with their mouths taped depending on the demands of their program and training phase.

Mouth taping works because breathing through the nose creates and releases nitric oxide, which widens the blood vessels and delivers more oxygen to your lungs and circulatory system, allowing your body to generate more energy and work more efficiently. On the other hand, breathing through the mouth does not have this effect, which means the cells don't get as much oxygen as they should, which can lead to fatigue and stress.

So what are you waiting for? Give mouth taping a go!

THE POWER OF 'BOX BREATHING': UNLOCKING YOUR POTENTIAL

In today's fast-paced world, it's hard not to feel overwhelmed, stressed and anxious. Work, family and personal demands can all negatively affect our mental and physical health. But what if I told you there's a really simple technique that will help you manage your stress, improve your focus and enhance your overall wellbeing? It's called 'box breathing'.

Box breathing, also known as 'four-square breathing', is used by athletes, yoga enthusiasts and even military personnel to manage stress, anxiety and increase performance. It's a basic yet incredibly powerful technique. Just follow these five steps:

1. Breathe in slowly through your nose, counting to four. Feel the air enter your lungs.

2. Hold your breath for four seconds.

3. Slowly exhale through your mouth for four seconds.

4. Pause at the bottom of your exhalation for four seconds.

5. Start the cycle again with another slow inhalation, and repeat for as long as you want.

The benefits of box breathing are numerous. Similar to the other breathing techniques we've discussed, box breathing stimulates our parasympathetic nervous system, helping to calm our mind and body. When this relaxation response is activated, our blood pressure, heart rate, and the level of stress hormones in our body are all lowered. Box breathing also increases the oxygen flow to our brain, enhancing our concentration and cognitive performance.

Incorporating box breathing into your daily routine is straightforward. You can do it anywhere, anytime and for any length of time. Just find a quiet space, sit comfortably, and begin with a few deep breaths. Inhale for four seconds, hold for four seconds, exhale for four seconds, and hold for four seconds. Repeat the cycle for a few minutes, gradually increasing the duration. Consistency is key; practising box breathing daily is key to maximising its benefits.

Box breathing is a valuable tool for athletes and fitness enthusiasts as it helps improve endurance, performance and recovery. By regulating our breathing, we control our heart rate, conserve energy and reduce fatigue. Box breathing can also be used as a pre-workout ritual to increase energy, focus and motivation.

In addition to its physical and mental benefits, box breathing can also enhance our social and emotional wellbeing. Reducing stress, anxiety and the effects of depression improves our relationships, boosts our confidence and increases our sense of fulfilment. Box breathing, like the other techniques mentioned earlier, can also help us connect with our inner selves, increase our self-awareness and promote spiritual growth. It's a powerful holistic tool that I use a lot in my workshops to help people unlock their potential.

So, take a deep breath and give box breathing a try. You'll be amazed at the difference it will make to your life.

6.
MEDITATION – BE AT PEACE, GET IN THE ZONE (WITH TOM CARROLL)

I've been meditating on and off since I was about 17 years old. But in the last 10 years or so I've really doubled down and have been meditating every single day. It's now an integral part of my mental and spiritual routine. In this chapter I'll explain why meditation should be an important part of your path to longevity too. To help me out, I'm excited to have my good friend and mentor, two-time world surfing champion, Pipe Master and all-round legend, Tom Carroll, along for the ride. At the end of the chapter, Tom will talk about his journey and what he's learned from his many years of meditating.

Meditation has profoundly affected the way I see, experience and appreciate the world. It's helped me understand when to step up and when to pull back; how to let go, accept and embrace change; and how to mindfully deal with the inevitable challenges that life throws our way. Through meditating, I've learned how to get into a 'flow state' and smile at life's difficulties, as well as how to connect with my emotions on a deeper level – and even transcend them. Meditation has benefitted my energy levels, my sense of happiness and tranquillity, my self-esteem, and my understanding of both myself and the world around me. The anxiety and depression I often experienced, particularly in my thirties when I was so busy building my business, working with clients and running classes, has slowly eased thanks to meditation. My focus has improved, along with my working memory. I can now access beauty and transcendence whenever I sit down and let go. Even my motivations make more sense.

But meditation is no magic pill. It's a lifelong practice that, with determination and patience, will help you peel away the layers of self and ego. But while it may seem pretty simple on the surface – and of course meditating costs nothing – committing to it does take a little bit of time and effort. The good news is the journey can begin for you today, and the results are immediate.

Just as we must overcome all sorts of challenges when we decide to change what we eat or how we exercise, the start of your meditation journey will be fraught with obstacles. Before you can meditate, you need to quieten your passing thoughts and feelings, navigate your emotions, and learn how to ignore the incessant noise of life. It's not easy! You have commitments, demands on your time, family obligations, friends who need you, bills to pay, and maybe a career to manage. You might be experiencing addiction or a mental illness that is interfering with your life. There's just so much that can disturb us and prevent us from finding that quiet space. Think about your particular situation and your day-to-day life: what are your main distractions? What keeps you from being able to sit down and tune out the world?

Once you've worked out what's distracting you – and how you might free yourself from those distractions – it's time to begin. But where to start? There are many different types of meditation, deriving from many different traditions, but they all have one thing in common: they all offer a direct path to better mental and physical health. Choose a style of meditation that's right for you, one that is appropriate for your current struggles and aspirations. You are more likely to stick with it if it works *with* your life and yields results, rather than making your life more complicated.

Where did I begin? While I'd meditated on and off since I was a teenager and knew a bit about what was involved, when I decided to fully commit, it was hard going. I knew it would take a long time (a lifetime!), but I was determined. I started with baby steps – just five minutes a day for the first six weeks using a popular meditation app called Headspace. After six weeks, I built up to 10 minutes a day, still using the app, and I kept this up for another 12 weeks. Then I moved to 15 minutes for another 12 weeks. After a year I was meditating for 15 minutes each day, every day. The following year, my goal was 20 minutes, but now it would be a *self-guided meditation* – without an app or calming music! It took me another 12 months or so to learn how to maintain a meditative state for that length of time. I had to train my brain to be clear, and not get distracted by rogue thoughts. Perseverance paid off: today I meditate for at least 20 minutes a day. Every day. Tom Carroll inspired me to make that 20 minutes as deep and profound and transcendent as possible. So long, 'real world'!

For those who aren't familiar with the term, 'transcendence' just means to go or climb beyond the range or limits of normal, ordinary human perception and experience. It's often described as a spiritual or religious state of mind, or a condition of moving beyond physical needs and realities.

Here are some of the apps I used when I began meditating regularly:

Insight Timer: this app contains a free library of over 120,000 guided meditations; ideal for anyone who's new to meditation. The app's meditation and mindfulness exercises are aimed at managing stress and anxiety, as well helping us to get deep, quality sleep.

Calm: this app talks you through many different approaches to mindfulness and meditation and also includes a library of soothing sounds, ambient music, 'sleep stories' and masterclasses. The app is useful for both novices and regular practitioners, and it helps us reduce stress, manage anxiety and practise self-compassion.

Breathe: this app has similar functions to Calm, and emphasises sleep solutions, including hypnotherapy for deeper, more restful sleep.

Headspace: this app's motto is 'meditation made simple', and it guides you through the basics. It tracks your progress so you'll be encouraged by the length of your meditation and the effects it has on your vital signs, and it sends you reminders to help you stick to your routine.

(You can also try a couple of meditation series on my new app: **Holistica Academy**.)

Out of the four apps mentioned above, I found that Headspace worked best for me as it employs a straightforward design. I could set time durations, goals and reminders. There wasn't as much talking as the other apps, so it was easy to follow. While I don't use the app anymore, I'm so grateful to have had it at the start of my meditation journey.

Meditation is like any other training or sports practice; you must put in the time to get better and train your brain. Remember, what you do *every day* matters far more than what you do *occasionally*. Meditation is no magic pill and you will find it hard when you begin. The results will come, I promise you, but it'll probably take longer than you think. So be patient and stick with it.

WHY SHOULD I MEDITATE EVERY DAY?

In today's busy world, stress is unavoidable. Sadly, many of us also struggle with depression, anxiety and other mental health issues. This means that our sleep, cognition and physical and mental wellbeing can quickly deteriorate. Problems can overwhelm us, and many people lose focus. In time, our health worsens, and our determination starts to flag. The best medicine to combat all of this that I've found is meditation. And what's more, it's free!

Countless studies have now shown that meditation helps reduce stress. It also regulates our emotions and improves our ability to concentrate. It has a positive effect on our cognition, specifically in our frontal and limbic systems and brain function, especially the 'insular cortex', a small portion of the cerebral cortex, which is involved in our emotions. Long-term meditation helps preserve brain structure and function and ultimately contributes to greater longevity. On a more metaphysical level, meditation can move us towards a state of 'pure consciousness', where our minds are completely empty of thought.

Meditation establishes and then strengthens the connections between the mind, body and spirit. It helps you achieve balance, a state of relaxation and equanimity, self-control and discipline. It also raises and develops consciousness and awareness. You will be able to deal with life's adversities better than before, when you might have responded to situations with anger, or let fear or anxiety affect your decisions and relationships. I know that's promising a lot, so don't let the thought of meditating 'the right way' add any more anxiety. Meditation can be as formal or informal as you like; the important thing is that it suits your particular lifestyle and situation. So keep it simple, start with baby steps, and always remember to balance it with good nutrition, exercise and hydration.

Before we get into the nuts and bolts, it's useful to understand a bit of the history. After all, people of all cultures and faiths have been meditating for thousands of years. Its origins can be traced back to ancient Hindu and Buddhist traditions in India. In Hinduism, meditation was practised as early as 1500 BC and was known as *dhyana*. It was used as a means of calming the mind, withdrawing it from the world of external sensations and achieving a state of deep relaxation and inner peace. In Buddhism, meditation was used to achieve spiritual enlightenment and liberation from the cycle of birth, death and rebirth. The Buddha, Siddhartha Gautama, meditated and taught his followers various techniques.

Meditation also has roots in Taoism, Confucianism and other ancient Chinese traditions. In Japan, Zen Buddhism developed a unique form of sitting meditation, known as *zazen*. Meditation has now moved beyond its religious origins and has become a widespread practice for improving mental and physical wellbeing.

There are many different types of meditation, each with their own techniques, aims and benefits. The main benefits I'm interested in centre around becoming more mindful of the present in order to counteract the modern mind which is consumed by busyness, anxiety about the future, and general stress. As we've discussed, all this negativity can have a disastrous effect on your physical and mental wellbeing. Meditation brings us back to the present, so that we can enjoy the miracle of the moment and be attuned with our family, our friends, our community, and the world around us. Additionally, meditation will help you build resilience in the face of adversity and trauma by improving the way you regulate your emotions.

I've found the philosophy of Taoism of particular use. 'Tao' is commonly translated as 'the way' or 'the path', and relates to the natural order of life, an eternal truth. Taoism aims to help us manage the constant flow of change, and place ourselves in balance and harmony. The basis of Taoism, as put forward by Lao Tzu in the foundational text, *Tao Te Ching*, presents the following three pillars as a way of navigating life:

Simplicity: when you are *simple* in your reactions and thoughts – meaning when you're humble and without affectation – you return to an eternal source of being.

Patience: being patient means being able to accept or tolerate delays, problems or suffering without becoming annoyed or anxious.

Compassion: this is our capacity to recognise the suffering of others and then take action to help.

Other principles of Taoism include:

Going with the flow: in Taoism, the less you need to force things, the sooner you arrive at a place of stillness, tranquillity and 'non-action'. According to Lao Tzu, 'If nothing is done, nothing is left undone.'

Letting go: this concept is hard for many people, but if you accept that everything in life is in a constant state of change, you'll let go of rigid expectations. Believe in your path and trust the process. Don't try to anticipate everything; keep your routine and commitment going.

Harmony: this is about organising the parts of your life into a whole that is consistent with existence's greater nature and order.

Breathe: take time to be grateful for your life and the people around you. Be open to listening and learning new things – you are never too old to do this. Masters are those who are open to listening to everyone and anything without judgement.

THE BENEFITS OF MEDITATION

The benefits of meditation are almost too many to mention! Here are just a few:

Increased self-awareness. Meditation can help you become more aware of your thoughts, emotions and behaviour, which will lead to greater self-understanding and personal growth.

A lower resting heart rate. This is particularly important for performance in sport and general longevity. A moderate, steady heart rate means your heart is unstressed, strong and working efficiently.

A new perspective on stressful situations. Meditation reduces stress and anxiety by calming the mind and promoting relaxation. When you reach this place of stillness and calmness, you'll find it easier to put life's inevitable ups and downs into perspective.

Increased focus on the present. Regular meditation brings you into the moment – the now – rather than dwelling on the past or feeling anxious about the unknown future. Being in the moment allows you to focus and concentrate on the tasks at hand.

Better immunity. Studies have shown that meditation can improve immune function and reduce inflammation. When I'm stressed, my immunity becomes fragile and my blood counts drop. Meditation helps counter this.

Fewer negative emotions. Meditation increases our feelings of happiness, wellbeing and contentment. You become more patient and tolerant of opposing ideas and general day-to-day frustrations.

Improved imagination and creativity. Meditating quietens the inner critic and self-consciousness that prevents the free flow of creative energy. Once we begin to explore our inner self, we'll discover the talents that hide behind the wall of ego.

Improved sleep. Regular meditation helps filter out the worries that keep you awake at night and burden your subconscious. This deepens the quality of sleep and reduces insomnia.

Lower blood pressure. Meditation can help lower blood pressure and in turn reduce the risk of heart disease and other conditions.

Better management of chronic illness. While meditation won't cure serious illness, it can help you navigate the pain, anxiety and confusion surrounding conditions like depression, panic attacks, cancer, chronic pain, irritable bowel syndrome and tension headaches.

I'm often asked what the difference is between meditation and mindfulness. Meditation and mindfulness are two related but distinct practices. Both have become very popular in recent years. While there are similarities, they are unique activities with several key differences.

Mindfulness is *living actively* in the moment and being fully aware of sensations, your surroundings and the emotions running through you. When you're mindful, you observe your thoughts and feelings from a distance, without judging whether they are good or bad. You can practise mindfulness informally, through everyday activities like eating, walking, brushing your teeth, riding the bus or even having a conversation. Mindfulness is a bit like slowing down the movie of your life so you pay full attention to what's really happening. You're fully engaged with the flow. Your executive functions (like memory, attention span, organisation, self-discipline and planning) improve. Once you've experienced the benefits of mindfulness, you plant the seeds for more such moments to come.

Meditation, on the other hand, is the practice of quietening the mind (sometimes by focusing on one particular thought, idea, object or phrase to direct your attention to a specific point). A key principle of meditation is *concentration*, where you put yourself in an environment in which the noise of the outside world is reduced. That doesn't mean meditating on a mountain top! A quiet place at home, a park bench, or an unused office at work will do. The quietened mind then lets go of distractions and allows us to tap into our inner wisdom and clarity. Meditation can certainly teach someone to live a mindful life!

BEING 'IN THE ZONE' – ACHIEVING A 'FLOW STATE'

You may have heard people – athletes, artists, dancers, writers, knitters, rock climbers, and so forth – refer to being 'in the moment', 'in the zone' or in a 'flow state', but what exactly do they mean? Essentially, they are searching for the following:

- A state of consciousness where your skills perfectly match the requirements of whatever you are doing
- The ability to totally concentrate on the performance of that activity, without distractions
- A hyper-focused, sometimes spiritual state of mind where anything is possible and where we start to be extremely productive, creative and powerful.

When you're 'in the zone' everything seems to 'click'. You feel like there are no limits to what you can do. We all have skills and ability levels in certain activities. And we also have expectations on how those skills translate to 'performance'. For example, if we've spent a lot of time surfing, we tend to know what we're capable of. Sometimes, we develop an expectation that we aren't able to meet. We can get psyched out, intimidated, allow fear and anxiety to creep in, become scared of letting ourselves and others down, or afraid of success, or allow past disappointments to infect our present selves – there's just so much going on beneath the surface that can affect our performance!

We get into the zone (or flow state) when our skill level precisely matches what our ideal performance is in our mind, once all those limitations are transcended. This state of altered consciousness allows us to perform at our very best and achieve amazing results. The Greek philosopher Plato wrote about the 'state of divine inspiration', which could be achieved by creating harmony between the mind and body. Our fears are overcome when we achieve this harmony, and the mind and body move as one. You can focus on the details of the task and the mechanics of the body (hello, mindfulness!), and nothing can disturb your attention and discipline (hello, meditation!). With this heightened sense of concentration, you'll perform at your peak. And epic results will follow!

It's important to note that this mental state cannot be forced or 'turned on' with a click of your fingers. It only comes when you've put in the hard yards, raising your skill level, and then matching that with the work you've put in to disciplining your mind and freeing it up so you have a clear vision of what you want to achieve. Then, when the conditions are favourable, you will rise to the occasion naturally and achieve a flow state.

There are a couple of things you can do to prepare yourself. First and foremost, as we've discussed in previous chapters, it is essential to practise regular self-care: getting enough sleep, exercising often, eating organic and nutritious meals, taking breaks throughout the day, breathing correctly and setting aside time to meditate. This is essential for achieving optimum performance. Second, you need a clear vision of your goal. Visualisation is a powerful tool that can encourage and motivate you.

Nothing worthwhile in life is easy and entering a flow state requires focus, determination, commitment and *consistency*. It turns out that even 'letting go' isn't as easy as it sounds! Getting in the zone takes time and practice. However, once you learn how to access a flow state, you'll be able to remain there for longer and longer periods of time. As your skills improve, you'll find that being in the zone is not only an incredibly productive experience, but it's also a deep one. You'll be able to see past the curtain of your ego and self-limiting beliefs and tap into your true, unvarnished, active, beautiful self.

Despite its elusive nature, there are certain techniques that athletes use to help them get into the zone. You can modify these depending on what works best for you.

Visualisation: athletes often picture in their minds their desired outcomes before they practise or compete. Doing so helps them to focus on what they want to achieve and allows them to put all distractions aside.

Positive self-talk: we know what it looks like when an athlete melts down under the pressure of the moment, berates themselves and can't contain their frustrations. To stay in the zone, athletes need to remain positive, motivated, focused and resilient when challenges arise. This can be achieved through positive self-talk or repeating positive mantras (for example, a powerful word, phrase or sound).

Music: listening to music, or even an inspirational podcast or a favourite audiobook, can help athletes get into the zone. The rhythm of the music helps generate a sense of flow and can remove some of the anxiety before competing. Music can also connect us to positive past experiences or memories when we performed at our best.

Breathing exercises: as we discussed in Chapter 5, slow, deep breathing reduces stress levels and allows athletes to focus more on their performance and less on their anxieties. This is not only true for athletes; breathwork helps anyone with commitments or tasks that are mentally or physically strenuous.

Get lost: it's important to allow ourselves to 'get lost' in an activity, completely giving ourselves over to its movements and rhythms. When this occurs, our ego and self-limiting beliefs take a back seat and we pay attention only to what's in front of us.

Achieving a flow state can be especially beneficial for people in high-pressure jobs. It can help increase productivity, sharpen focus and allow creativity to emerge. A flow state enables individuals to access their subconscious, just beyond their awareness, from where most creative ideas and solutions come. Even though it's largely hidden, the subconscious is a deep well full of potent visions, hopes and dreams. We must bring those to the surface, access their raw power and live them out in the conscious world. That's how a person's performance can surpass the level of their conscious efforts.

To achieve a flow state, you need to engage in an activity that is enjoyable yet challenging. It must be attractive enough to keep the competitive fire in us burning, but if the task is too easy, the goal too readily obtainable, boredom can set in. Conversely, if the task is too complicated, frustration can take hold and make you want to give up. So it's essential to find a balance between challenge and capability.

You also need to focus on specific goals or tasks in order to minimise distractions. We need clear objectives with measurable results. Charting your performance over time will provide tangible feedback and allow you to control how you spend your attention and energy in order to improve.

In the end, we're all striving to live an authentic life, be true to ourselves, and achieve our dreams and goals. But sometimes, we let them go because we think we aren't made for it, or our time is up, or our glory days are over. The art of longevity is about embracing the richness and flow of the moment – the *real* moment – at any point in our life and holding on to that feeling for as long as possible.

If you follow the tips in this chapter, you'll soon begin realising your potential and elevating your health and wellbeing. Meditation opens the gates to the self – with a bit of practice, anyone can do it, and it's free! Getting into the zone – a flow state – enhances your performance in whatever field you're in. And don't forget to reward yourself for your successes. Celebrating your accomplishments will give you an extra boost and remind you why working hard is worth it.

TOM CARROLL'S STORY

I fell into recovery from drug addiction in 2006. Playing a major role to this day is close involvement in 12-step fellowships. In the eleventh step it suggests we 'seek through prayer and meditation to improve our conscious contact with a God of our own understanding, praying only for the knowledge of its will for me – and the power to carry that out'. When you've been doing lots of drugs on a daily basis, you feel powerless to stop. You *can't* stop. You eventually get to a point where you need to surrender to something greater than yourself.

Other people in the recovery program seemed very calm. They'd been clean for many, many years. I couldn't imagine being clean for more than 24 hours! Seeing these people who'd been clean for so long, and who had this inner calm, had a profound effect on me. They could listen. They were collected and able to talk and laugh and carry on. They had this way of being that I wanted. One of the guys was really into meditation. I wanted to turn off the noise in my head, which was very loud. When I quit all substances on 18 December 2006, I needed the tools to stay sober.

Meditation became one of the main tools in my recovery.

I learned that meditation has to be a daily practice. And so I did it every day, with guidance from others in the program. I soon began to see the effects. I was promised that if I continued I'd learn how to recognise the gap between my first thought and the action that follows that thought. The addict can't recognise that gap; you just give yourself over to your first thought. You say to yourself, *I'm just going to do whatever my thinking says, and then I'm gone* . . . When there's no gap between our first thought and action, we are incapable of seeing our mistakes as they happen. Because our thoughts present as so dominant and so realistic without any gap for awareness, we become prone to incoherent actions, random and crazy along with our thoughts. In fact, our thoughts are not random – they come from somewhere deep within us, a reservoir beyond the mind.

I didn't know any of this when I began meditating. But I put my faith in those who'd been doing it for a long time and looked to be in pretty good shape. And that's what I wanted. *I* wanted to be in good shape. The challenge for me was sitting with myself in the unknown. I didn't know what it was like to be with myself. At first it was uncomfortable sitting for much more than five minutes. Five minutes was a very long time for me back then. I had an unsettled nervous system. I was agitated all the time. And on top of that, I'd welcome stress into my life. I brought stress into my body, brought it into my nervous system, because I thought that was the way you had to do life.

But the older, clean members in the recovery program encouraged me to stick with it. They encouraged me to get up in the morning, wash my face, sit down, put myself aside and let god in. Those were the instructions. It was so simple. 'Don't tell me "but" or "just", I don't care. Sit.' 'You got ADHD? Sit.'

So I said, 'Oh, okay. I'll just sit.'

After a while, thanks to my achievement mindset, having competed in surfing for so long, I started thinking, *Oh, I'm going to get to 30 minutes. I'm going to get to 40 minutes. I'm going to get to 50 minutes!* It was insane. I was still trying too hard, putting in too much effort. But I started to experience the benefits. I became calm. I was more able. I could manage my relationships more effectively. I was able to *be*. I could see myself doing all sorts of things in the future, functioning.

I could also step back and realise, *Oh, I would've done that before, but I'm not doing that now. Something's going on here. I'm feeling more settled. I don't have to do all this other stuff that I think I have to do.* It's so important to have this self-realisation, and for me it was brought about by regularly sitting by myself in the morning, before the day started.

So this is how my meditation path began – a mindfulness, breath-based style of Tibetan Buddhist meditation – and it became my path for 10 years.

Eventually, I drifted off course. I was down to 10 minutes, just lying in bed. I realised something was going on. I realised I needed this. Meditation had been very beneficial. So I reached out through prayer and asked, *Can you please show me how to enrich my meditation practice?* Within days, I met up with a Vedic meditation teacher in Avalon, near where I live on Sydney's Northern Beaches. I enrolled in a course. I realised that teacher was there for a reason.

The Vedic tradition involves 20-minute meditation sessions twice a day, so you really have to step up. I grew strong during that course; it gave me a powerful reason to put my hand up and get more involved. In 2018, about a year and a half in, my Vedic teacher said to me, 'Tom, you have to teach.'

'But I'm not a teacher,' I said.

He persisted, 'Tom, you *must* teach. You're a true teacher. You must see where it leads.'

'Nah,' I replied.

Now I'd like to see him again. Because the truth is I have helped some people along the way. Vedic teachers help people with their recovery. I know my life changed because of it. It was a nice feeling, seeing that happen naturally over the years. But to actually charge someone money to do a course? I struggled with that, and still

do. But then I thought, *Why not? Let's do the teaching course.* So I sat the course to become a teacher in Vedic meditation and began in 2020, when the COVID-19 pandemic had us all in lockdown. Imagine that – a substance-abusing former professional surfer teaching Vedic meditation!

The Vedic tradition is about 8500 years old. It's a tried and tested technique handed down from the masters who looked into the true nature of themselves and developed and built on their practice. This is not some iPhone app that you update. We're talking about the human condition here. When we look into the nature of reality, we see it through the lens of our consciousness. Consciousness is how we perceive things. Depending on your state of consciousness, this is how you view the world. We all have our own unique state of consciousness. I can't change yours, and you can't change mine. And I don't want to rely on belief here. We need to go for experience. I'm not trying to give you a religion. I'm not trying to tell you what you have to believe. Go for your own direct experience of yourself.

The Vedic masters went deep and looked into the nature of reality. And they came up with these beautiful techniques. In the transcendental style of meditation, we use what we call a *Bija* mantra. *Bija* means seed. This means it's a mantra that's not outwardly spoken but inwardly thought. And this mantra uses thought vibration. Sound complicated?

We know Nikola Tesla was an extraordinary human being, an electrical engineer who looked into the science of electricity and vibration. He thought if you wanted to look into the nature of reality, look to vibration, energy and frequencies. What happens when we have lots of thoughts running through our mind, and they're all really, really loud, and we're full of stress in our nervous system and general physiology? Our make-up starts to change. We start to deteriorate. Our system starts to break down on a cellular level.

What do we do when we don't have anything in our life that allows us to return to our true self, that offers us the chance to experience ourselves in the least excited state? Regular meditation practice can bring us to a stillness, a centre, which is supreme inner contentedness. If we don't have experience of ourselves in this contented state, we're probably overdoing it, because that's the way our lives are lived today.

That's why meditation is more relevant now than any other time in human history – we've never been so besieged by information, competing for our time and attention. And we've convinced ourselves that we need all this information. We go into 'acquisition mode', and then we can never get enough. We become fixated on the confusion. We get lost. This is a typical human experience. We think we're just a human *doing*, rather than a human *being*. And so if another person's not doing what we're doing, we don't think they're human! We actually look at them like they're not even a human being, when we're the ones who have forgotten.

Everyone else then becomes the same. And then we're really on shaky ground. The Vedic masters knew about this, but their technique used to be quite exclusive. You had to trek into the Himalayan mountains and find a teacher, and that journey might take three or four weeks. And then the teacher might look at you and say, 'Oh, come back in a month. Do this one practice every day, and then come back in a month. And then I might teach you.'

I've been asked about my goals in teaching meditation, and the only one I really have is to bring as many people as possible into the experience. That's my drive. I had to be crazy driven to become a world champion surfer, but this is a different type of drive, a different type of sensation. If your need is strong, but you think that you can't meditate, get someone to guide you. We all need teachers and we all need to be open to learning. We can't graft a new idea on to a closed mind. Let's open up to the possibility that someone may be able to help you to get beyond yourself and go to the unknown.

Meditation is a beautiful way to offload stress. It's a beautiful way to experience ourselves as human *beings*, not human *doings*.

Ultimately, I just want to be who I am, fully, and keep evolving. If I did have one goal for myself, it'd be to build on my ability to consistently bring good judgement into my life.

7.
CONNECTING TO THE ENVIRONMENT AROUND YOU

We are currently facing an existential threat due to the horrific effects of climate change. Pollution, deforestation, devastating bushfires, loss of jungles and other vital habitats, shrinking ice shelves, rampant urbanisation, degraded oceans . . . The list is endless and it's easy to feel overwhelmed and lost. How can humanity have got it so wrong? What disaster is next?

With so many threats to our very existence, it's more important than ever that we stay connected to the environment – that we respect it and are grateful for it – and that we allow it to work its magic and positively affect our health and longevity. Like any relationship, we must not neglect it: we need to make a conscious effort to *nurture* it.

It's only by being *in* nature that we truly connect *with* nature, learning how it works and our place within it. Appreciating the part we all play generates gratitude and awe, and from that comes a greater sense of personal responsibility and a desire to protect. We develop a better understanding of how we can live in harmony with the natural world and reduce our impact on it. Through this deeper connection we come to see ourselves as *part* of nature, rather than *separate* from it. To harm nature is to harm ourselves; to heal nature and enjoy it is to heal and nurture ourselves – physically, mentally and spiritually.

By actively engaging with nature, we encourage others to do the same, while simultaneously reaping the benefits. That's why connecting with nature is crucial to any discussion of longevity. Whether it's incorporating bush walks and ocean swims into your routine, or practising meditation and breathwork by the beach, or by just going to a park and sitting and switching off from technology during your lunch break, every time you engage, you're making an active decision to lead a healthier life and limit all that can constrain our lives.

There is truly no downside – humans have always existed (and evolved) according to the laws of nature – and whether we're learning about plants and animals, or being part of community initiatives like clean-ups or planting native plants, connecting with nature is one of the best things we can do not only for our physical and mental wellbeing but also for the planet. It doesn't take grandiose gestures: small acts can make a big difference.

Have you ever felt overwhelmed despite doing all you should for a balanced and healthy life? Do you exercise regularly, manage your diet, and stay on top of sleep – but still feel disconnected from your environment? Have you found you've ticked all the boxes of what modern society tells us is important for good health but are still feeling a void, a lack of energy or a disconnect with the world around you? If this is the case, put on your hiking shoes, or grab a surfboard, or put on your gardening gloves and get outside. Engaging with your natural environment might be the missing piece in your journey to holistic health and longevity.

I'm regularly asked what I mean when I talk about 'engaging with the environment'. Engagement is when you combine respect for the natural world with outdoor activities that you enjoy in order to generate positive feelings and a sense of awe. If you see your favourite beach spoiled with litter, cans and rubbish on an otherwise beautiful day, you might take a rubbish bag and gloves on your walk with friends and help clean it up. You might join a trail running group with people who share your enthusiasm for nature and are respectful and encouraging of one another. You might visit a community farmers' market rather than the supermarket and meet the people who grow your fruit and veggies. You'll make more responsible choices with your money, and have a laugh with the locals in the process! Harmony, joy, a sense of wellness and tranquillity, and gratitude for the work of others come from engaging with nature.

Here are a few practical tips to get you started.

- Take time out every day to appreciate the natural world. Combine this with your exercise or meditation routine. You could stop and sit by the ocean, a river, or just watch the rain. You could take a moonlit walk. Nature, weather, birdsong – it's everywhere you look! You just need to go and meet it, whether it's racing out the door with a paddleboard or cracking your window when a storm rolls through.

- Plant flowers, herbs, succulents – anything! – in pots on your windowsill, balcony or patio to bring a touch of nature into your home. Pot plants introduce colour, vibrancy and maybe even birdlife to your surroundings. I live in an apartment and have a collection of bonsai trees on my balcony. I love to spend time every morning watering them, shaping them and feeling their energy.

- Join a community garden or gardening club and learn about native plants or how to grow vegetables and herbs. There's nothing more organic – or more rewarding – than growing your own food.

- Connect to the wildlife around you through birdwatching. Buy a field guide and see how many species you can identify. Become an expert on the birds in your local area.

- Embrace your inner activist. Attend an event that promotes environmental awareness in your community. Volunteer at a local conservation project to help make a positive impact. Pick up litter wherever you see it!

- Stargazing on a clear night will give you a sense of awe and connection to the cosmos beyond our planet. Sometimes it's good to feel small!

As an avid surfer and a part of the professional surf community, I am blessed to be able to spend a lot of time in nature, observing the action of the water, and marvelling at all the sea creatures. Being in nature not only brings out the best in our sporting performance, but it brings the best out in our personalities as well. The ocean is not just an escape from our busy lives but an opportunity to connect, learn and expand our minds. Every time we paddle out it's an exciting adventure – our brain and body are firing, we experience a sense of freedom, and we appreciate the beauty and wildness around us.

Surfing also means choosing different locations, reading the weather and looking for new breaks and new experiences. I've been lucky enough to travel to distant islands and learn about different cultures. Each environment is stunning in its own way; it has its own unique vibration and energy, and plants and animals.

Here's how engaging with the environment can improve your longevity:

- Studies show that spending time in nature can lower your blood pressure, which improves your overall fitness and reduces the risk of heart disease.
- Like meditation, connecting with the environment positively affects your mental health by reducing stress and anxiety, lowering your heart rate, and promoting creativity.
- Connecting with nature gives you a greater sense of purpose and meaning. Studies show that people who feel connected to the natural world are more likely to protect it. This sense of purpose is one of the key contributors to longevity and leading a more fulfilling life.
- Nature's calming effects create a sense of balance by providing a refuge from the hustle and bustle of everyday living. For most people, paying attention to nature's sights, sounds, scents and textures is completely different from being at work.

- Research has shown that people who spend time in nature experience improved circulation, increased energy levels, healthy weight management, better sleep patterns, improved attention spans and better memory recall.
It makes sense! When we are in nature, we are surrounded by beauty and countless new stimuli, which keeps us engaged, stimulates our brain and forges new neural pathways that being indoors simply can't.

I'm thankful I've always lived close to nature – my house as a kid in Brazil was surrounded by parks, and on the weekends I got to go to our beach apartment, or to our cottage in the hinterland. As I grew older, my goal was to live even closer to the beach, preferably somewhere with perfect waves. Today, I'm blessed to call stunning Coolangatta on Queensland's Gold Coast home. My apartment is about 200 metres from one of the best point breaks in the world, Kirra Point, and my clinic is only 700 metres from another famous point break, Snapper Rocks! I couldn't be more grateful for being able to connect with nature right outside my door.

THE IMPORTANCE OF CONNECTING WITH THE ENVIRONMENT FOR ATHLETES

Despite their incredible feats, athletes are still human and need to cultivate meaningful connections with nature just like the rest of us. Pro surfers, rock climbers and mountain bikers all still need to connect with the environment in order to maximise performance, remain healthy in the long term and keep injuries at bay. At the elite level, sport and lifestyle cross over in healthy ways. There's good reason why most surfers tend to have a positive mindset, a sense of balance and a sense of peace when they're in the water. And don't forget the old saying, 'A bad day on the slopes beats a good day at the office!'

For those athletes who must compete indoors, getting outside allows them to take a break from their training regimes, reset and come back stronger and with a better perspective. But regardless of whether we're an elite athlete or not, we all can use a break! Particularly when you're injured, you need to slow everything down, and getting outside will give you the space to recalibrate.

Connecting with nature can also help athletes prevent injuries by improving their coordination, stability, mobility and agility while also building their overall strength and endurance. Anyone who has cross-trained by sprinting up sand dunes, battling through breakers or tried paddleboard yoga to improve their performance in another sport will know what I'm talking about! Nature provides a special energy that is sympathetic to our own body's natural vibrations; this relationship helps athletes stay focused on their goals and maintain good mental health. We should never misjudge the energy and strength of nature, and humans are still learning how to harness this effectively.

HOW NATURE HELPS YOUR WELLBEING

So many of us live our lives in fear: fear of judgement about our 'status' in the world; fear of the opinion of others; fear of the future; fear of doing those things we love because we don't feel worthy; fear of change; fear of the moment. Observing the natural world around us can help offset such fears and allow us to appreciate life more deeply. For me, when I'm surfing – reading the sets of waves coming in on the horizon, feeling the movement of the water around me, observing the ebb and flow, marvelling at the marine life – I am totally in the moment, unworried about the past or the future.

There are many ways that being in nature benefits our wellbeing:

Stress reduction: being in nature helps reduce our levels of cortisol, the stress hormone.

Improved mood: spending time in nature improves our mood and reduces symptoms of anxiety and other disorders. Nature provides a sense of awe and wonder. Our problems can be put into context which helps us feel more positive and uplifted.

Increased physical activity: getting outdoors and getting moving connects us to nature in a way that humans have done for aeons. It's our natural state and activates our bodies and minds – and don't forget the 'stoke' that comes with outdoor sports!

Better sleep: natural light helps regulate our circadian rhythms, releasing serotonin – the chemical that controls our moods, emotions, appetites and digestive system. At the end of the day, darkness releases melatonin, which settles us for a good night's sleep. Being active outdoors during the day means we'll have a restive night, where our body recharges and vital cells regenerate.

Enhanced cognitive function: being in nature sharpens our cognitive functions, such as our attention, focus and memory. Our worries fade; we're in the moment.

Improved immune system: being in nature boosts your immune system and improves overall health. Non-threatening micro-organisms abound in nature, and by ingesting them – by breathing or swallowing them – our immunity is strengthened and is better able to combat more serious threats.

PRACTISING APPRECIATION AND GRATITUDE

Perhaps the best part of immersing yourself in the beauty of the natural world are the feelings of appreciation and gratitude, two important emotions we must actively promote and bring into our daily routine. After all, nature provides the essential elements for our survival – water, sunlight, the nutrients in the soil that come through in our food, the insects that fertilise our flowers, the fungi that decomposes organic life. How could we not be grateful for that!

Every morning after meditating, I go out onto my balcony and express my gratitude for the beauty around me and all that I have. I appreciate how lucky I am to be alive. When you focus on the good things and express gratitude for them, you shift your focus away from negative thoughts and emotions. This helps to reduce stress and anxiety. Gratitude is a mindset that can carry you positively through your day.

Let's examine these two concepts in a bit more detail.

Appreciation

The dictionary defines 'appreciation' as 'the recognition and enjoyment of the good qualities of someone or something' and 'a complete understanding of a situation'.

Appreciation is about noticing the little things in life – the beautiful details, the small threads in the tapestry that make up the whole. It's hard to fully appreciate life unless you immerse yourself in the daily small miracles that are continually happening all around you. When this occurs, your focus and attention become so acute that even the smallest incidents can bring you pleasure. Your body and senses are literally absorbing the world around you, digesting it and drawing wellbeing from it.

Practising appreciation engages the mind and fires up the brain's synapses. We begin to see the world in a new way. We are more inclined to notice the good things and value them.

Of course, 'appreciation' can mean different things to different people. Some people appreciate the value of being thrifty and living a sustainable life that benefits nature, the economy and society at large. Others appreciate personal achievements – the incredible advances humans are capable of, or just being our best selves. While others appreciate relationships, or the power of music, or comedy and laughter. The power of protesting about a cause you believe in helps some people appreciate community and our ability to effect change.

Appreciation allows people to focus on what they have rather than what they lack.

There are so many ways to practise appreciation: you can keep a gratitude journal, you can be intentional about expressing thanks to others, you can incorporate appreciation into your meditation routine, or you can simply open the door, walk outside, open your eyes and smile.

Showing appreciation for others, acknowledging their positive qualities and the effect that they've had on our lives, gives us a greater sense of connection to our community. Our empathy gets a workout; we feel the joys and pains of others and are able to stand in their shoes for a moment. Research has shown that people who regularly practise appreciation experience increased happiness, better physical health, improved relationships, and greater resilience in the face of adversity. If you cultivate a positive mindset and focus on the good things in your life, you'll improve your overall wellbeing and lead a more fulfilling life.

Gratitude

While appreciation is the recognition and understanding of the positive things in our life and the way they influence us and shape the way we see the world, gratitude is the *active expression* of that appreciation. Gratitude is often expressed for those things in our immediate circle: our family, friends, children, the food on our table, our home. But it can be expanded to so much more, such as the miracle of being and the universe itself. Most of us focus our gratitude on the positive aspects of our lives and acknowledge the good things that we have; but we can also be grateful for the challenges that have made us, that have taught us lessons, that have allowed us to triumph over adversity and flourish.

Gratitude isn't about long-winded declarations, elaborate displays of emotion or expensive gifts. Gratitude is free. It can take the form of a few simple words, a mantra, a note to a friend, or it can just be a feeling, or a warmth in the heart.

Researchers have begun studying the science of gratitude, helping us to work out exactly what goes into our physical, emotional and mental wellbeing. Their findings suggest that practising gratitude can actually alter the structure and function of the brain, leading to highly beneficial long-term changes in our thinking and behaviour. It's a beautiful circle: the more grateful I am, the more beauty I see and the happier I become.

'When you are grateful, fear disappears, and abundance appears.' TONY ROBBINS

Some people have described gratitude as a sort of 'social glue' and key to building and nurturing relationships. A study of early adolescents showed an association between gratitude and its ability to enhance social cohesion, encourage support for others and engender empathy for the welfare of those who are struggling. One fascinating result showed that boys in particular benefit from practising gratitude. They also greatly benefit from receiving support from their family – where their strengths and their weaknesses are discussed on a daily basis. Simple expressions like 'I'm proud of you', 'I'm inspired by you',

'I'm excited to see where this opportunity takes you', 'I love you and want to put the pain of the past behind us' can have a hugely positive effect.

Other studies show that being grateful brings a variety of benefits that contribute to our longevity, improved physical performance and better mental health. We actually live longer, more meaningful lives if we regularly practise gratitude! We are more motivated by others, we enjoy the dance of life, our stress levels are reduced along with our heart rate and blood pressure. We're more inclined to exercise and we experience less fatigue during our workouts. Furthermore, those who are grateful tend to experience fewer aches and pains as they age – gratitude gets you moving (walking with friends who fill your cup, going to the beach to watch the sunrise, riding your bike to work so you can appreciate the world around you rather than endlessly checking your social media).

Grateful people tend to be less stressed, have fewer head-aches, sleep more soundly, are less fatigued and have better digestive health since their sympathetic nervous system (fight or flight response) isn't getting constantly triggered. Instead, the parasympathetic nervous system (the system that allows the body to rest and digest in peace) is more engaged. We've already discussed the connection between the gut and the brain. Peace of mind helps your organs function properly and positively affects your overall physiology. Peace of mind can lead to a healthier gut. Remember, everything is connected.

Some people can find it difficult to speak from the heart. Maybe they're shy, self-conscious, or fearful of sounding odd or being rejected. But true gratitude is liberating: the ego shrinks, people are empowered being around you. Gratitude is like a muscle, once you start exercising it, the more naturally it comes and the more strength it develops. Gratitude doesn't have to involve words – you can express it with a smile, a laugh, a high-five, a thumbs up, or even a silly emoji!

So take time each day to express your gratitude for all that you have. I practise gratitude in the morning when I wake up and at night before I go to bed. Sometimes gratitude just washes over me after a midday surf, leaving me with a big smile that I carry with me through the rest of the day.

It's so easy to focus on the things you don't have in life, the opportunities that you weren't presented with, the sometimes unfair or random events that lead some to succeed and others to fail. It's hard to be grateful when you're surrounded by problems, when you don't feel 'blessed' or life has taken away something or someone you love. But even in loss you can still feel gratitude for the impact a person's life has had on you, or the next door that is going to open, or the chance to start again. We all must learn to savour the good moments when they come along and not take them for granted.

Here are a few tips on how to practise gratitude:

- Say a simple expression like 'thank you' or 'I appreciate you' to someone who has done something kind or helpful.
- Be grateful for the love and support of your family and friends.
- Express thanks to someone who has provided you with guidance or mentorship, whether it's through a challenging situation or in pursuit of your goals.

- Take a moment to look around and appreciate the beauty of nature – sunlight coming through your window, the movement of the clouds, the insects flying about your garden, birdsong, stars in the night sky.
- Feel grateful for the opportunity to learn and grow, whether through education, travel, books, music, food or other life experiences.
- Feel gratitude for the health you have at whatever age you are, the ability to engage in physical activities and hobbies you enjoy.
- Express gratitude before going to bed each night – you'll sleep more soundly and have better dreams!
- Be grateful that you have endless opportunities to make a positive impact on the world and the lives of those close to you.
- Acknowledge the efforts of your work team and colleagues, and express gratitude for their contributions to a project or meeting.
- Recognise and be grateful for the small, everyday things we often take for granted, such as a warm cup of tea, a hug, a good meal, a good night's sleep.

Benefits of practising gratitude include:

Improved mental health: gratitude has been shown to reduce the effects and symptoms of depression, anxiety and stress. Gratitude opens the door to emotions like happiness and contentment.

Improved physical health: gratitude benefits our sleep and blood pressure, reduces inflammation in the body, and improves our immune system and heart health.

Better relationships: when you express gratitude to others, it increases feelings of connection and empathy, and helps strengthen your relationships. You're more inclined to show forgiveness, to trust, to be yourself, to feel empathy and to work for the welfare of others.

Increased resilience: practising gratitude helps you build strength and cope better with challenging situations.

Gratitude can be a powerful force in shaping our attitudes, in opening the door to different perspectives and experiences. We become an active participant in the goodness in our lives; we live more joyfully. Your mind and heart open, and you see not only 'the big picture', but also the millions of everyday miracles happening right in front of you.

8.
COMMITTING TO RECOVERY

If you're serious about your longevity – and you've begun practising all of the healthy habits and routines outlined in the previous chapters – then you also need to commit to the practice of *recovery*. Whether we're talking about your physical, mental or emotional wellbeing, the importance of healing, of regaining your strength, and of allowing your body and mind to reset and stay on track over the long haul cannot be overstated. In fact, recovery is just as important as physical and mental training, and nutrition, but it's often the element that's least talked about.

In the short term, proper recovery will mean improved performance during competitions or workouts due to less DOMS (delayed onset muscle soreness). DOMS is that pain and fatigue you often feel a few days after a workout or strenuous activity. In the long term, proper recovery will ensure good mental health by reducing stress, minimising the risk of injury and helping you build strength.

Unfortunately, I had to learn about the importance of recovery the hard way. For many years, while I was at uni and when I was travelling the world, I regularly worked 10 to 14 hours a day, pushing my body and mind to the absolute limit. Not only that, I was getting minimal sleep (four to six hours a night). I thought that was the pathway to get ahead and achieve my goals. We live in a culture that values the relentless 'grind', whether it's in the gym, the classroom or the workplace – and there's no shortage of people out there who'll encourage you to go down this path! But by behaving in this way, I ended up repeatedly injuring myself. I ended up having two knee surgeries, bulging discs, shoulder pain, a couple of severe bouts of the flu, not to mention heaps of stress and emotional turmoil.

Thankfully, I managed to navigate this period by doing the exercises I've explained earlier, therapeutic sessions on a foam roller, stretching routines, and paying close attention to what I was eating. If I hadn't done all that, my condition would have been a lot worse.

Perhaps the most valuable thing I learned from that time was the importance of getting adequate, restorative sleep. It's so simple – and doesn't cost a thing! If you don't get enough sleep, you lose muscle mass; you burn less fat, making managing your weight difficult; and you slowly wreck your body and mind. It sounds crazy and counterintuitive, but it's true. Sleep is absolutely fundamental for our mental and physical wellbeing and essential for performing at a high level. It's probably the most basic – but most important – step when it comes to recovery.

Recovery should be a *priority*, not an *afterthought*. Investing in your healing must be a part of your daily routine – as critical an activity as exercising, meditating, eating well and getting out and about in nature. And remember, what you do *every day* is more important than what you do *occasionally*! If you follow the recovery tips in this chapter, you'll soon see improvements in your performance, strength and overall wellbeing.

Before we get into the key elements of recovery, here's what you need to do first in order to put yourself in the right frame of mind.

ACKNOWLEDGE THE IMPORTANCE OF RECOVERY

The first step is to fully appreciate why recovery is so important. The fact is most people don't. They need to pay *more* attention to the value of rest, relaxation and replenishment. They wrongly believe pushing themselves to the limit is the only way to succeed. But as I found, relentlessly grinding away will only set you back and run your body into the ground. It will lead to burnout, injury and frustration when you plateau, or even start going backwards. In order to thrive in the long term, you must accept that recovery is just as important as any other part of your journey towards greater longevity. Practising good recovery is not a sign of weakness but a sign of wisdom.

CREATE A RECOVERY PLAN

The next step is establishing a clear and effective plan. This means identifying the areas that need attention and developing strategies to address them. This might include regular massages, stretching, foam rolling, meditation, hydration, good nutrition, adequate sleep and social support. It might include more complex recovery protocols which I outline later in this chapter. The main thing is, by having a structured routine for recovery, you make it a priority in your life.

KEEP TRACK OF YOUR PROGRESS

Monitoring your progress is essential for staying committed. Whether you use a journal, a fitness tracker, an app or a coach, keeping a record of your recovery efforts, your results and your ongoing challenges will keep you motivated and on track. You'll see how far you've come, where you need to improve, and how far you have to go. This awareness will give you a sense of accomplishment and fuel your determination to keep going.

STAY POSITIVE AND BE COMPASSIONATE WITH YOURSELF

Maintaining a positive and compassionate mindset is essential. While allowing your body to heal during your training regime is critical to preventing injuries in the first place, you can't always avoid getting hurt! Life happens. Accept that setbacks and obstacles are all part of the journey and that you're not alone in facing them. Be kind and patient with yourself, especially during periods of stress or pain. Instead of beating yourself up over a missed workout or a bad day, focus on your progress and how to bounce back. Celebrate the small victories and your efforts to improve your life. You're on a path that has peaks and valleys.

SEEK HELP WHEN YOU NEED TO

Finally, don't be afraid to ask for help when you need it. Whether it's from a therapist, a trainer, a coach, a friend or a support group, reaching out will give you the boost and guidance you need to stay on track. Don't let pride or shame stop you from getting the help you need to heal and grow. Remember that we all need support sometimes, and asking for it is a sign of strength, not weakness.

Committing to recovery means you're taking a decisive step towards achieving your goals and living your best life. Acknowledging the importance of rest and replenishment, creating a recovery plan, tracking your progress, staying positive and compassionate towards yourself, and seeking help when you need it will mean you stay motivated and in the best place to overcome challenges. Remember that recovery is not a one-time event but a lifelong journey.

Now we've covered the 'why' of recovery, let's examine the 'what' – treatments ranging from the most basic, to those that are at the cutting-edge of medicine.

MASSAGE THERAPY

All athletes know how vital muscle recovery is to performance. There are many different ways of achieving this, and adequate sleep, nutrition and hydration are just the start. Why don't you consider adding massage therapy to your recovery routine? The benefits of massage therapy include:

Reducing muscle tension and soreness: after a challenging workout or competition, muscle soreness and tension are common. It can last for days, delaying your recovery time. There are many types of massage: deep tissue (targeting inner muscle layers and connective tissue); trigger points (releasing pain and tension in particular 'knots' in your muscles and fascia); and sports massage (addressing the parts of your body that bear the load or impact of a particular activity) to target areas of soreness and stiffness, lessen muscle tension, and promote blood flow. The manipulation of soft tissues like muscles, ligaments, tendons and the fascia helps to reduce inflammation and alleviate muscle pain.

Enhancing flexibility and mobility: if you're a gymnast or a competitive dancer flexibility and mobility are critical to your performance. But even if you're not competing, massage therapy will improve your flexibility and mobility. A skilled therapist can use techniques like myofascial release (the tissues surrounding and supporting your muscles) and joint mobilisation, which can help to break up adhesions (scar-like tissue), reduce muscle tightness and enhance range of motion.

I like to mix massages into my mobility training because it precisely targets the fascia and network of 'sling' muscles that connect various muscle groups that give us stability, releasing tension. I'm very particular with my massage regime, but it's important to understand that one single massage won't solve the problem. Find a protocol that suits your needs and goals and stick with it.

Boosting blood flow and nutrient delivery: the muscles and surrounding tissues undergo stress and damage during an intense workout. Recovery requires delivering oxygen, nutrients and fluids to those stressed areas to restore natural function and range of motion. Massage therapy increases blood flow and stimulates the circulatory system, quickening your recovery time.

Relaxation and stress reduction: recovery isn't all about the body, though! It's essential to consider mental and psychological recovery as well and massage therapy is an effective way of relaxing and reducing stress. Swedish massage, which targets the top layers of muscles with soothing movements and tapping, and aromatherapy (the treatment of minor conditions, by rubbing pleasant-smelling natural substances into the skin or breathing in their smell), help trigger the release of serotonin and dopamine, promoting relaxation, happiness and better sleep. Sometimes you need deep-tissue treatments to release pain and tension in trigger points and ease inflammation; other times you just need to relax and let everything go! It's important to balance both.

Mindset control and performance: your mental approach to your performance influences how you recover physically. Massage therapy can help your mental and psychological recovery because it stimulates the parasympathetic nervous system, which activates the 'rest and digest' response, allowing the mind to relax and clear out any stressors. So, massage also has an impact on our gut and nervous system, boosting immunity and organ functions.

Many people associate massages with indulgence or see it as an unnecessary expense. The reality is it's an effective tool that humans in all cultures have been practising for thousands of years. And there are plenty of affordable practitioners to suit your budget. Massage recovery can be a game-changer for anyone looking to maximise their performance, longevity, training and mindset. For those who haven't experienced the benefits firsthand, why not give it a try?

If I have a particularly active period at work, like training lots of clients, implementing their routines and working across different sports simultaneously, I try to have one massage a week for 6 to 10 weeks. After that, I reduce the number to one massage a fortnight. I've found I need that balance to keep my body whole and life and career on track. I honestly can't go a month without a massage! The main reason is the bulging discs in my back, particularly the one in my thoracic area. If I start getting tight and allow the pressure to build, it will annoy me for months until I get a massage and release the tension.

If you have muscle inflammation, are experiencing pain in tight areas or trigger points, and moving poorly, start with

6 to 10 massage therapy sessions (one per week). As soon as the tightness and pain starts to ease, and your movement starts to improve, reduce the number of massages to one every fortnight, letting the body adapt, and then move to once every third week or once a month for maintenance. Just don't let it go longer without a treatment or you'll risk relapse.

SAUNA THERAPY

Saunas have been used for hundreds of years in Scandinavia. The word 'sauna' comes from the old Finnish word 'savuna', which translates to 'in smoke', though historians think that saunas actually date back centuries to ancient Greece, the Roman Empire, and the Indigenous people of Finland. In recent times, the practice has attracted a lot of attention from the medical community due to its health benefits, particularly how it enhances recovery.

Saunas can reduce inflammation and stress, improve sleep, and even lower your risk of developing specific medical conditions. Regularly having a sauna has been linked to increased physical endurance and improved cognitive functioning. And frequent sessions can elevate your mood and relaxation levels.

Sauna therapy involves sitting in a heated room, typically at a temperature of 45 to 90°C. The heat causes the body to sweat, which dilates the blood vessels and allows more oxygen and nutrients to reach the muscles. This increased blood flow helps remove waste products like lactic acid, which can contribute to muscle soreness and fatigue. Sauna therapy also stimulates the parasympathetic nervous system, which induces relaxation and reduces stress. This then promotes better sleep, which is essential for recovery.

Aside from the physical benefits, having a sauna also helps your mental and emotional wellbeing. Sauna therapy promotes the release of endorphins, the body's natural feel-good hormones, which improve focus and mood, and reduce anxiety. The relaxation induced by the heat helps release mental tensions, leading to a clearer, calmer mind.

For athletes and fitness enthusiasts, sauna recovery is beneficial in improving performance, as it helps reduce muscle fatigue and soreness. By improving blood flow, the heat from the sauna stimulates muscle recovery, which can help increase strength and power output. It also facilitates metabolic processes, which aid in the growth and repair of muscle tissues. As a result, athletes see increased endurance, quicker recovery times, and better overall performance.

Lastly, sauna therapy has been linked to increased longevity because it can lower the risk of developing cardiovascular diseases. Time spent in a sauna has been found to help reduce blood pressure, which is a leading cause of stroke and heart disease. One study found that those who spent time in a sauna had fewer instances of heart disease and a lower overall mortality risk. In addition, sauna therapy has been shown to improve insulin sensitivity, which is necessary for regulating blood sugar levels and reducing the risk of diabetes.

Sauna therapy is an excellent addition to any recovery routine. Many gyms now have saunas on site, and some dedicated spas offer regular sessions. Start with a 20- to 45-minute session, with the temperature somewhere between 45 and 80°C. The best time to have a sauna is after training, in the afternoon or night-time.

One important reminder: don't forget to drink heaps of water, before during and after, and even take an electrolyte if you need to. Your kidneys will be working hard to keep you hydrated and flush out impurities, but dehydration stresses the kidneys through overuse. Remember: hydrate, hydrate, hydrate!

ICE BATH RECOVERY

Ice bath recovery (also known as cold-water immersion or cryotherapy) has been big in the health and fitness world for quite some time now. It might sound crazy, but taking a dip in freezing water helps athletes recover faster, reduces soreness and physical tension in overworked muscles, and improves longevity.

The technique involves exposing your body to icy water for up to 20 minutes. The water temperature is usually between 10 and 12°C, though some people opt for a more intensive treatment, going one to four minutes maximum at 0 to 5°C, and sometimes longer.

A bit like a sauna, the benefits of an ice bath are more than purely physical – ice baths help improve your mindset by taking you well outside your comfort zone. By pushing through the discomfort, you learn more about your physical limits and culti-vate mental toughness. It feels counterintuitive to put yourself into such a cold, confronting environment for your own good, but when you do it, you prove to yourself the extremes you're capable of enduring. You get a new idea of what sort of discomfort you can tolerate and the seemingly impossible circumstances you can overcome.

On a physiological level, ice baths cause the blood vessels to constrict which reduces inflammation and speeds up muscle recovery, allowing you to get back into top shape much faster. Ultimately, it is up to the individual to decide if an ice bath is right for them, but it's hard to deny the potential benefits of regular use. Even an ice-cold shower in the morning produces a similar effect. Give that a go first.

Depending on the temperature of the water, aim for three weekly sessions of two to four minutes each. Research shows that ice baths are most effective at 5°C with two to four minutes of immersion rather than 12 to 14°C for longer periods. It's also important to note that ice baths are recommended for general body maintenance and *not* recovery from acute injuries, like sudden trauma in a particular joint or muscle. For those sorts of injuries, it is essential to use hot therapy to help muscles relax to get functionality back for proper healing.

HYPERBARIC OXYGEN THERAPY

No matter our level of fitness, we all experience the after-effects of physical exertion, from workout-induced soreness to twinges and sprains caused by accidents or overuse. These discomforts often linger, and life becomes more difficult and painful. Athletes are after efficient, non-invasive therapies to jump-start rehabilitation, accelerate healing and improve performance. Hyperbaric oxygen therapy (HBOT) can address many of these issues.

What *is* hyperbaric oxygen therapy?

HBOT involves inhaling 100 per cent pure oxygen in a pressurised chamber. The air we breathe under normal conditions contains about 21 per cent oxygen, which is filtered through the lungs and carried to cells by the bloodstream. However, more oxygen reaches the bloodstream, tissues and organs when we breathe it under high pressure. And this accelerates the healing process.

How does HBOT work?

HBOT works by forcing pure oxygen to dissolve quickly into the blood plasma and tissues, where it stimulates healing. The therapy can affect all parts of the body, from the brain to the muscles, the bones to the organs.

Who can benefit from HBOT?

HBOT can benefit a wide range of individuals, including those recovering from surgery, injuries or other medical conditions such as strokes, heart attacks or infections. Athletes use HBOT to speed up recovery, reduce inflammation and pain, and prevent injury. For people in good health, HBOT can improve immunity, boost cognitive function and enhance energy levels.

What are the specific benefits of HBOT?

Reduced inflammation: it delivers oxygen to inflamed areas, helping to reduce swelling, redness and pain.

Enhanced wound healing: it accelerates collagen production and stimulates the formation of new cells, leading to faster wound healing.

Improved brain function: it increases cognitive function, improves memory recall and boosts creativity.

Accelerates injury recovery: individuals who have sustained an injury can use HBOT to accelerate their healing process and return to activity faster and at optimal performance.

HBOT is a promising and effective alternative to conventional medical treatments. It is a reliable therapy in sports medicine and injury recovery, it enhances longevity and performance, and improves your mindset. The therapy is cutting-edge science, so requires a specialist's supervision for optimal results. If you are interested in trying it, talk to a health professional first. They'll help you decide if it's the right therapy for you. If you decide to proceed, the HBOT protocol is much like the other therapies mentioned earlier. Start with 10 to 20 sessions (one per week), depending on your issues, and reduce it to once per fortnight and then once every month.

PEMF THERAPY

PEMF (pulsed electromagnetic field) therapy has been around for over 50 years and was first used by NASA to help astronauts manage the physical challenges of space travel. Since then, it has been clinically shown to support recovery, improve overall wellbeing and enhance athletic performance.

What is PEMF therapy?

PEMF therapy delivers low-frequency electromagnetic waves to cells and tissues to regulate and enhance cellular function. It improves blood circulation, boosts cell metabolism and reduces inflammation, which can help the body heal itself naturally.

How does it work?

PEMF therapy devices rely on electromagnetic coils to deliver electromagnetic pulses to the body. These pulses mimic the natural electromagnetic frequency of the Earth, which helps to energise you at a cellular level. When activated and energised, your cells work more efficiently, enhance cell metabolism, improve circulation and stimulate overall healing.

What are the benefits of PEMF therapy?

PEMF therapy can improve your recovery time from various ailments, such as sports injuries, surgeries and age-related illnesses. It can also help athletes recover from physical stress and improve their performance. Some of the many benefits of PEMF therapy include reduced inflammation, improved immune system function, increased energy and improved sleep.

In addition, it can also help combat depression and anxiety. The electromagnetic pulses stimulate the release of endorphins and other feel-good hormones, promoting a sense of calm and wellbeing. Last but not least, PEMF therapy really helps your frame of mind! Research has shown that it enhances performance and resilience in stressful situations. It also improves cognitive performance, boosts attention, and helps with mental clarity and focus.

If you're looking for a natural, non-invasive way to support your recovery, improve your physical performance and enhance your overall wellbeing, PEMF therapy might be right for you. It is safe, effective and non-invasive, making it a great choice for those who prefer to avoid taking medications or undergoing invasive procedures.

I have a PEMF machine at home and use it regularly. It helps me regulate my system and balances my energy levels. At night, it eases me quickly into my parasympathetic system and helps me get a deeper sleep.

We humans can't help pushing ourselves to the limit. We chase our dreams, tackle complex challenges and persevere through tough times. However, our bodies often pay the price for our ambitious pursuits, and we experience pain, inflammation and injury, particularly as we age. For those who find conventional recovery therapies ineffective, there are several innovative, more experimental therapies available that may help us bounce back from such setbacks. In recent years, peptides, PRP and stem cell therapy have gained popularity among athletes and others who wish to optimally perform and then recover. It should be noted that the science behind these treatments is still evolving, so before considering any of them, please consult a qualified healthcare professional who'll assess your needs and determine whether they're right for you.

PEPTIDES

Peptides are short chains of amino acids that play a vital role in the body's physiology. Certain peptides have emerged as potent tools for recovery, and have been shown to accelerate wound healing, improve gut health and reduce inflammation. Others have been used to improve muscular endurance and accelerate tissue repair, and promote sleep quality, which is an essential pillar of recovery. Peptides are administered through injections and are generally considered safe under most conditions.

PLATELET-RICH PLASMA

Platelet-rich plasma (PRP) is a therapy that involves taking a sample of an individual's blood, processing it to concentrate the platelets and re-injecting it into the injury-affected area. Platelets are critical for blood clotting but also contain growth factors that stimulate healing and tissue regeneration. PRP has been used to treat injuries including tendinitis, muscle strains and osteoarthritis.

STEM CELL THERAPY

Stem cells are the body's 'building blocks', the only cells that are able to make different cell types, like muscle, blood and bone. Stem cells can also be used to fix damaged tissue. They're incredibly powerful and are part of an exciting new branch of medical research. Stem cell therapy involves harvesting the cells from your body (autologous) or from a matched donor (allogeneic), processing them and injecting them into the injury-affected area. The therapy has been used to treat injuries, such as ligament tears and rotator cuff injuries, and degenerative conditions, such as osteoarthritis. Stem cells can enhance tissue healing and regeneration, reduce inflammation and improve joint function.

COMBINING THERAPIES

While these cutting-edge therapies all have unique benefits, in certain circumstances they can be combined to amplify their effects. Combining peptides, PRP and stem cell therapy, for example, under the guidance of a qualified healthcare professional, may provide even better results. People who have done so report faster recovery times, increased energy and an overall improvement in their quality of life.

All these therapies offer promise for enhancing our body's ability to heal and regenerate after injury. Of course, the techniques are still evolving and being tested, and we're still learning how they affect the body and mind. However, they definitely offer hope for those who've exhausted conventional medical treatments and need to explore other avenues. Remember always to consult a qualified healthcare professional first.

THE 'OPTIMAL' VIEW OF RECOVERY

As much as anything else, recovery is a mindset, an approach to training and life that emphasises rest, rejuvenation and the long-term benefits of your efforts. Recovery is a process, not a moment. It's not enough to rest for a day or two and expect your body to magically heal. Recovery is *active*. It requires participation and involves rest, hydration, nutrition and other critical factors. It's not just about the time you take off but how you use that time to support your body's natural healing processes.

Mindfulness and intentionality are key

Optimal recovery also means approaching your rest period with *mindfulness* and *intentionality*. What do I mean by that? Well, instead of scrolling social media or binge watching Netflix, take the time to reflect on your training, set yourself goals, and visualise your progress. Incorporate activities that promote relaxation, such as yoga, meditation or a walk outdoors. Taking a mindful approach to recovery will help you recharge physically, mentally and emotionally.

Recovery is part of performance

Recovery is not just about feeling better after a hard workout; it's also essential for improving performance. When you rest properly, your body repairs damaged tissues, replenishes your energy stores and builds strength and endurance. Without proper recovery, you risk overtraining and burnout, ultimately hindering your performance. Optimal recovery means recognising that it's an integral part of your training program, not just an afterthought.

Longevity and recovery go hand in hand

Optimal recovery is central if we are to achieve longevity. You don't have to be a professional athlete to know that training takes a massive toll on your body. By taking a holistic approach to recovery, you will improve your performance and ensure that you can continue to train and move without pain for years to come. Remember, recovery isn't just about the short-term gains; it's about setting yourself up for a healthy and active life over the long term.

Optimal recovery is personal

Finally, optimal recovery is *personal*. What works for one person may not work for another. What your friend recommends may not suit your body's needs or help you achieve your goals. Different activities and lifestyles require different approaches. Common to all of these approaches, though, is a mindset that prioritises rest to balance activity, focuses on the rejuvenation of the body and mind, and is dialled into the long-term benefits of your training. By viewing recovery as a holistic process and incorporating mindfulness and intentionality, you will enhance your physical, mental and emotional wellbeing long into the future.

Experiment with different recovery strategies, listen to your body and find what works best for you. The simple treatments work well and most of them don't cost the Earth. If you feel you need something more sophisticated, talk to a qualified health professional. Whether it's a rest day, a massage, a sauna, a cold plunge pool, a hot bath – or one of the more experimental therapies – *prioritise* your recovery. You won't regret it!

HERE'S A SUMMARY OF MY RECOVERY PROTOCOL

Massage: once a fortnight, sometimes once a week when I'm doing extra work.

Sauna: two to four times a week. I am really lucky to have a sauna at home, which helps me fit it into my weekly schedule.

Ice bath: two to four times a month. I don't have my own ice bath, so I go to a recovery centre or use a friend's. My goal is to eventually have my own at home and be able to do it at least two to four times a week.

PEMF therapy: three to five times a week. I have a machine at home and find it helps a lot, although it is a significant investment!

9.
THE ART OF LONGEVITY – MAKING THE CONNECTION

If you've made it this far in the book, you're probably thinking the whole concept of longevity is pretty complex. You might be thinking that achieving it involves a radical rejig of your entire existence. Well, in part, that's all true, but don't be scared: while the journey to longevity is challenging, it's totally worth it!

Longevity is a deceptively simple word that at its most basic just means 'living for a long time'. Old age is something most of us don't like thinking or talking about – maybe that's because most of us decline physically and mentally as we get older. Our quality of life deteriorates and we decay. But it doesn't have to be this way. By implementing the strategies outlined in this book, by taking a mindful, patient and consistent approach to how we move and think, what we eat and drink, how we recover, and how we interact with our community and our environment, we not only give ourselves the best chance of living a *long* life, but also living a *quality* life.

Remember: what we do *every day* is more important than

what we do *occasionally*. Of course, genetics, lifestyle factors, environmental conditions and access to medical care all play a part in our longevity journey too. Many of these factors are out of our control, which is all the more reason to pay special attention to those factors we *can* control.

We all want a long and prosperous life, but let's aim to be those people who get to enjoy a long, prosperous and *active* life – surfing, travelling, biking, hiking, doing whatever you love – going beyond the point where some say, 'I'm too old for that! Those days are over!' After all, who wants to spend their time whining about ill health and saying, 'Remember when . . .'? Let's instead aim to be those people who say, 'What's next?'

As I've tried to demonstrate throughout this book, in order to do that, we must *consciously* and *intentionally* make healthy choices. We have to establish new routines and deliberately steer clear of all of those unhealthy habits and mental traps that stop us enacting the vision we've created for ourselves. When I was younger, I worked hard and overcame my health issues. I learned new ways of living – and I'm still learning – and I'm now reaping the rewards. If you commit to changing your life and follow the tips in this book, you will too.

Here's a breakdown of what we all need to do.

CUT OUT THE BAD HABITS WHERE WE CAN AND BE OPEN TO LEARNING NEW ONES

Quitting or limiting our bad habits helps us cleanse our system and opens our mind to new ways of living. I'm not just talking about drinking alcohol, smoking or drug abuse, eating junk food or indulging our cravings – these habits certainly contribute to chronic disease and reduce our quality of life – I'm talking about those ways of thinking that are just as toxic to our emotional and mental wellbeing. Taking stock of our lives, reducing (or even better eliminating) bad habits, and then establishing good habits is the first step on our longevity journey. Eventually these good habits will become automatic, which saves energy, time and unnecessary anxiety, helping us focus on the essential things in life. But first we need to take a good hard look at ourselves.

Recognise your bad habits

You need to recognise your bad habits if you want to end them. Bad habits can be anything from overeating, laziness, nail-biting or oversleeping, to neglecting sleep and binge drinking. These habits can wreak emotional and physical havoc, affecting your relationships, productivity and overall quality of life.

Write down your habits: which are destructive and need to be eliminated? How will you handle those bad habits that fight to stick around? Self-awareness is very important when it comes to recognising bad habits. Accepting who we are helps with our mindfulness and meditation routines, allowing us to lose the sense of 'self' and ego that often gets us into trouble.

I say this again because a lot of us don't accept our own bad habits and the barriers we place between ourselves and the vision we have. We often joke about our bad habits, to the point where they become part of our identity. If we don't take them seriously and see them for the existential threats they are, they'll stick around forever.

Replace the bad habits with new, healthy habits

After recognising, identifying and accepting your bad habits, the next step is to cultivate healthy habits, and incorporating them into your daily life in a way that will last. For example, instead of bingeing on snacks when you're stressed, try the meditation and breathwork exercises we covered earlier. They're simple and easy. Just close your eyes for five minutes and concentrate on your breathing – or go for a meditative walk outside your house or through a community garden or park. Exercising willpower will strengthen your resolve when it comes to confronting the next habit on your journey.

If procrastination is your bad habit, set clear goals with deadlines to help you focus on your tasks. Replace your bad habits with positive, healthy ones that promote physical and emotional wellbeing. Get up in the morning with a big smile on your face, think about how great you're feeling (even if you aren't) and how great your day will be (even if it's filled with difficult meetings or difficult people). As soon as positive thoughts take root and grow in your brain, you will start to train it to look for and amplify the positive things in your life. Disciplining your thoughts is like exercising your body – you must do it daily. Keep these positive thoughts in your mind; repeat them as soon as you open your eyes in the morning: *I feel good, my thoughts are focused on these good feelings.* Thoughts create feelings. Feelings create behaviour. Behaviours make and shape your day.

Never forget that mental health is an everyday practice.

Be open to those around you and create a support system

Be open and discuss any bad habits that are holding you back with close friends, family or even a psychologist. They'll help you identify triggers and maybe even help you to overcome them. It can be a scary, confronting step, but being open will create a support network, increasing your chances of developing healthy habits, and supporting your emotional and physical health. Support networks are an invaluable asset when we're learning new, healthy habits. But choose wisely; you need people around you who'll help lift you up, not drag you down.

Start small and don't panic!

It's easy to feel overwhelmed when you commit to changing your life. Incorporating healthy habits takes time, focus, patience and *practice*. One of the biggest mistakes people make is trying to incorporate too many changes at once. Take baby steps, and trust and respect the process. It always takes longer than you think, so don't panic as panic only leads to burnout and disappointment.

Start by choosing one habit you want to eliminate – or one habit you want to cultivate. Come up with a plan on how to tackle it, set realistic and achievable goals, and track your progress. It could be as simple as drinking more water or closing your eyes and meditating for five minutes. Once you have successfully incorporated the new habit into your routine, move on to the next.

Regularly refer to your written plan or checklist so you keep an eye on the path ahead. You'll see your intentions in front of you, broken down into achievable steps. For example, now that you're regularly hydrating in the morning and taking five minutes to meditate, add in some of the body movement routines from Chapter 2 to your morning routine. It is simple and achievable and can be done in 10 to 40 minutes depending on the time you have available. Feeling the boost to your energy levels, the dissipation of tightness in your body, and the fresh and happy mindset will inspire you to make further changes to your life.

Consistency is key

Always remember: true success doesn't come from some inherent greatness. It comes through a consistent pursuit of our goals over a period of time. Consistency is the key to longevity: as I've said again and again, what we do *every day* is more important than what we do *occasionally*. Consistent habits are the foundation of a strong and stable life and a strong and stable mindset. One of the big reasons people fail to cultivate new and healthy habits is that they give up too soon and go back to their old routines. Consistency is more important than perfection. If you find yourself getting off track, take a deep breath, pick yourself up and keep going. Stay positive and avoid self-criticism and judgement. The results will come!

If you follow these steps, you'll be well on your way to developing lasting, healthy habits, supporting your emotional and physical wellbeing.

Let's move every day, doing the activities we love

When pro surfer Kelly Slater talks about longevity, he stresses that he doesn't overdo things. He conserves his strength and energy so he doesn't get burned out. He trains for functional movement rather than going crazy with heavy lifting routines or intense cardio sessions, which can damage the body. He always has a reserve he can tap into.

Pushing yourself physically to the limit might give you results in the short term but it won't help your longevity. Work towards *functional movement* based on your specific activities to avoid burnout. Move every day based on your needs. You'll experience greater overall health: improved strength, flexibility and cardio capacity.

You've probably heard the phrase 'exercise is medicine'. Moving every day will not only benefit you physically, it will also help you mentally, increasing your memory and concentration. Even if you don't have time to hit the gym or go for a run, there are plenty of exercises you can do almost anywhere to help you stay fit and healthy. Regular physical activity will also give you a sense of accomplishment. You'll feel proud each day as you check off your movement goals and build long-term habits that will lead to a healthier future. The morning routine in Chapter 2 and 12-week training plan in Chapter 3 are great places to start.

Eat the best quality food that you can buy

Our diet is one of the most critical factors when it comes to longevity. A balanced diet is crucial for a healthy body. By choosing clean, organic wholefoods rich in nutrients, we fuel our bodies, reduce the risk of disease, and promote optimal health and wellbeing. Choosing the right foods nourishes your body *and* your mind. In Chapter 4, I explained some of the different diets you might want to try, depending on what's best for you.

Apart from the diets, here are some basic principles to follow.

Start by eating more fruits and vegetables! They're full of essential vitamins and minerals – and are delicious. Aim to eat wholegrains, lean protein and healthy fats. Avoid processed foods, which are high in sugar and salt and unhealthy fats. And avoid drinking too much alcohol. If you can manage these basic dietary steps, you'll be able to maintain a healthy weight, improve your cardiovascular health, and reduce the risk of chronic diseases such as diabetes and cancer.

Let's recap exactly what we should be eating.

Wholefoods: wholefoods are fruits, vegetables, wholegrains and organic lean proteins that are close to their original state, retaining all the natural nutrients that are often stripped away in processed or packaged foods. Processed foods are often high in sugar, salt and unhealthy fats, which increase your risk of obesity, heart disease and other chronic conditions. When you shop, make sure your foods are as close to their natural state as possible, and in season and local rather than imported.

Go fresh, go organic: I try to go to my local farmers' market at least once a week to buy organic fruit and vegetables. If I can't get to the farmers' market, I go to a good greengrocer. Not only does organic produce taste better than most of the stuff sold in the big supermarkets, it is also grown without synthetic fertilisers, pesticides and other harmful chemicals that are widely used in conventional farming. Not only that, organic foods are often higher in essential vitamins and minerals than their non-organic counterparts.

It's important to pay close attention to labels when selecting organic products, as not all organic items are created equal! If you're able to get to a farmers' market, make sure the produce is from small farms, where they don't use pesticides or other chemicals. Going organic is also great for the environment. Organic farming practices help to reduce those contaminants that can get into groundwater and harm wildlife. Organic farming also helps rebuild depleted soil health, which is essential for long-term, sustainable food production.

It isn't just about what you choose to eat but about making ethical decisions on *how* you want to live your life. We must be honest with ourselves when we shop. Simple changes to our lifestyle and eating habits can make a big difference to both our health *and* the environment.

Cook at home: going organic is more expensive, but cooking at home can help offset some of the costs. You'll have complete control over the ingredients you use and be able to experiment with different flavours and styles of cooking without having to pay someone else. Cooking at home is also a great way to spend more time with loved ones.

Read the labels: I know it's hard, especially when you're in a hurry, but most people don't read the labels on their food packages in supermarkets. It's a practice I learned at uni, and I was shocked to discover how companies mix in artificial additives and chemicals to make food taste a certain way – and get people hooked. It's really important to avoid foods that contain artificial preservatives, flavours and colours – those weird numbers you often see – all of which wreak havoc on your health. Also check for sugar levels, sodium (salt) levels, the amount of carbs and protein, where the ingredients come from, how and when the food's been produced, and the best-before date. The more you read labels, the quicker you'll be at deciding which foods to buy, which suppliers to support, and which ones to avoid.

Mind the mind for longevity

As we've discussed, longevity is about your physical health, and also your mental and emotional wellbeing. A healthy, stimulated mind increases life expectancy and limits the risks associated with cognitive decline.

Studies have shown a strong connection between our minds and our lifespans. Our mental wellbeing affects our physical health and vice versa. Other studies have shown that engaging in activities such as puzzles, crosswords, reading, writing, painting, and walks in new surroundings can help improve our cognitive abilities by providing a greater level of engagement with the world around us. Our brain changes and adapts to our surroundings. Engaging in complex problem-solving, acquiring new skills and participating in new activities keeps our brains sharp as we age by activating new neural pathways.

I always tell my clients, particularly those over 40, that we should never stop learning. We must keep challenging our brains and improving our motor skills. For those clients between 55 and 65, approaching retirement, I add they should never stop working, even if they try something different, perhaps community work or volunteering. If you don't keep your brain engaged, your mental faculties will deteriorate. So find new goals, invest in yourself and keep learning new skills. It will also keep you entertained and curious.

As we discussed in Chapters 5 and 6, incorporating meditation, breathwork and mindfulness into our daily life will also keep the mind sharp. We need to work hard to reduce stress, maintain a positive attitude and cultivate positive relationships.

We know how unmanaged stress can lead to health issues like anxiety, depression and chronic diseases. Stress is part of life, but chronic stress can have devastating consequences. It can lead to inflammation and a weakened immune system, and increase the risk of heart disease. So, wherever and whenever possible engage in activities that promote mental and emotional wellness.

As people age, they sometimes forget the importance of social connections and friendships, both of which are essential for good mental health. Humans are social creatures, and staying connected is vital for our longevity. A strong social support system reduces loneliness, stress, negative preoccupations and provides accountability. Our health suffers when we're isolated. Beyond your friends and family, engage with your local community. Connect with organisations that promote altruism.

Create an action plan

No matter what goals we set ourselves, whether they're personal or professional, we need to have a plan in order to achieve them. An action plan is a simple tool that will motivate you, put you on the right path, keep you focused and help you stay on track. Living a long and healthy life is the goal but we also want to feel happy and fulfilled along the way. As we've discussed, making lifestyle changes is difficult so we need an action plan if we're to succeed in the long run.

Elsewhere in this book, I've outlined some simple and effective plans that you can introduce into your daily life. Those plans aren't the endgame or the goal, but something to build on, mix up and improve as your mind, body and vision changes. Make sure to define your goals clearly at the outset. Be specific about what you want to achieve, and ensure your goals are measurable and achievable.

Committing to your action plan can be challenging, especially when things don't go as you expected or when you feel like giving up. During these times, try to stay motivated and remind yourself of your goals. Remember why you began this journey in the first place: to keep 'frothing' for a lifetime!

While action plans are important, we must also review the steps we're taking, how our body is adapting, and adjust the action plan accordingly. As you make progress towards your goals, you may find that your plan needs to be revised. Update your plan regularly to ensure you stay excited and engaged, and that your plan remains relevant and effective. Remember that having an action plan is a *dynamic* process, and you need to be flexible.

Understand and accept who you are — and be prepared to change

It's a hard truth, but a lot of people run from reality. Understanding and accepting who you are and the life you have is essential when it comes to the art of longevity. Yes, there are circumstances we cannot change or are born into. But acknowledging our limitations is an important part of moving forward and creating positive outcomes. Many of us go through life trying to fit in with society's expectations and norms, suppressing our true selves in the process. We feel pressured to conform to certain ideals of beauty and what a successful life looks like. We are forced into roles, often based on our gender or a perceived socio-economic 'class'. Certain personality traits are celebrated, leading us to mask our unique qualities if they don't conform with the mainstream. We try to be someone we are not. But living this way is exhausting and unfulfilling.

The key to living a happier, healthier and longer life is embracing the authentic *you* – understanding and accepting who you really are. It means being true to your feelings, values, beliefs and desires, and expressing them in ways that align with your identity. Taking time out to focus on self-care is important. Whether this involves sitting on a park bench and closing your eyes for 10 minutes at lunch, or signing up for a yoga class, or going on a walk in nature by yourself, or attending a week-long retreat, carving out time to understand *you* is vital. Seek out activities that help you clarify and understand who you are. Hopefully we'll come out of the process more patient and compassionate towards ourselves and others.

Another thing to note: self-acceptance isn't a one-off event – it is an ongoing process, taking in all the aspects of your life, and it requires consistent effort and dedication. Check in with yourself and your feelings, and admit when you need help.

When we embrace who we are without judgement or comparison, we more easily foster lasting relationships. When we know ourselves, we manage our unique stressors better; we improve our awareness of ourselves and others, and we build healthier habits that increase our overall health and wellbeing.

UNDERSTANDING YOUR AUTHENTICITY

Being 'authentic' means being true to yourself in your thoughts, words and actions. It involves knowing who you are, what you want, what matters to you – and then living life accordingly. So take some time to reflect on your values, and write them down. Ask yourself questions like:

- What makes me happy?
- What do I truly believe in?
- What am I passionate about?
- What do I stand for?
- What do I want to achieve in life?
- What are my core strengths and weaknesses?

When you explore these questions, you'll gain a deeper understanding of your authentic self, of who you really are. You'll start to recognise where you may have been suppressing or denying your true nature, or living counter to your values. Once you have a clearer sense of who you are, you can begin to live in a way that honours your authenticity.

There are countless benefits that come with embracing your

authentic self – for you *and* the people around you. It can lead to greater self-awareness and improved self-esteem, as you feel more grounded in your identity and less self-conscious about trying to fit into certain moulds or living up to imposed expectations. Your relationships improve since you are better able to communicate your needs, boundaries and values to others. People may disagree with you or deny you support, but this is okay: it's important to know who is truly part of your tribe. Being authentic will enhance your creativity, your resilience and your sense of purpose as you'll be more in touch with your innermost thoughts and emotions.

Embracing your authentic self is easier said than done; it can be very hard to accept and digest some of the changes and sacrifices that might be needed to align yourself with your true values. Embracing your authentic self involves confronting and overcoming all the fears, insecurities, limiting beliefs, prejudices and societal pressures that have held you back.

Here are some strategies to achieve this:

Practise self-compassion and self-acceptance. Be kind and forgiving to yourself. Recognise that it's okay to make mistakes or have flaws – we all do! Focus on your strengths, desires and passions, and be happy with your uniqueness.

Be mindful of your thoughts and emotions. Be aware when you are judging or criticising yourself (or others) and try to evaluate those thoughts in a more positive and empowering way. Feel your emotions without suppressing or denying them.

Set boundaries and prioritise your needs. Be clear about what you want and need in your life and communicate your boundaries to others. Make people aware. Don't burn yourself out by sacrificing your own wellbeing or values for the sake of pleasing others or conforming to society's norms.

Surround yourself with supportive people. Seek out those who accept and appreciate you for who you are and avoid those who judge or criticise you harshly. Join communities or groups that share your values.

Take baby steps towards becoming the person you were always meant to be. Focus on *progress* rather than *perfection*. Celebrate your successes along the way and learn from your setbacks.

TRUST AND RESPECT THE PROCESS: LONGEVITY IS OUR GOAL

Understanding and accepting your authentic self – and then making the necessary changes – is not a one-off event, but a lifelong journey of self-discovery and growth. By embracing your authentic self, you'll lead a more fulfilling, purpose-driven life, and inspire others to do the same. Remember that being true to yourself is not selfish or egocentric but an act of courage and integrity. So, take the first step towards authenticity today, and see how self-knowledge keeps us on the path to longevity.

10.
THE SAMURAI WAY

A big part of my lifelong journey towards longevity has involved investigating different sources of knowledge and wisdom from around the world. Once I started digging, I quickly found there are countless practices and traditions from other cultures that we can learn from here in the West.

I've already mentioned that I'm a bit obsessed with Japanese culture and traditions! I'm particularly interested in the ancient 'samurai code' ('Bushido' in Japanese) and how it advocates discipline, physical and spiritual health, as well as honour and compassion. While the code has its origins in late twelfth-century Japan, today it has become a lifestyle philosophy that is practised by millions of people around the world.

Traditionally, the life of a samurai was one of ritual and discipline. It was a life characterised by an unwavering dedication and tireless pursuit of perfection. It sounds extreme, but if we apply these principles to our own lives, they will help us to live more purposefully and establish positive, long-lasting habits.

In essence, the samurai code is all about taking charge of your actions, being focused, and methodically ordering the tasks required to achieve your goals. As we saw in Chapter 2 when we learned about routine and habit, many of us fail or fall short of our goals and give up too soon. This leads to disappointment. If we want to extend the meaningful, active years of our life, we *must* prioritise our mental, physical and spiritual health – and stick to the routines and practices to ensure that it happens!

The samurai code focuses on cultivating an unbreakable spirit, being courageous in the face of adversity, and remaining disciplined at all times. A follower of the code learns how to stay calm and composed when faced with the most difficult circumstances. They are able to focus on problem-solving and they never give up.

It's a way of being we can all apply to our daily lives and routines. It will help us deal with stress, difficulties at work, and everything around us; we will be prepared and mindful, and become calmer and more knowledgeable. The samurai prioritise self-care and practise mindfulness to maintain strength, balance and clarity.

BRINGING THE SAMURAI WAY INTO YOUR LIFE

Samurai culture placed great emphasis on maintaining a balance between the mind, the body and the spirit. They believed that the mind is the driver of action, and the spirit is the fuel. A clear mind allows you to let go and enables your actions to flow.

Practise discipline and self-control

Samurai warriors embraced discipline and self-control every day. For many of you, as we discussed in Chapter 2, this might be a challenge, but if you focus on your routine and breathwork, you'll get there. The samurai managed their emotions so they could remain calm and composed in the heat of battle. You too can do this – in your daily life, hopefully not in battle! Setting goals and timelines, and adhering to a schedule, will help you become more disciplined. Self-control means learning to tune out distractions and focus on your long-term goals.

Live a balanced life

When we think of the samurai we usually think of action on the battlefield, but they strived for a balance in *all* aspects of life – work, family, holistic health, spirituality and community. Focusing on one area at the expense of the others can quickly lead to burnout and exhaustion, a place many of us know all too well. Following the daily routines outlined in Chapter 2 will go a long way in building that balance into your life. You'll have time for exercise and rest; time for personal meditation and breathwork; and time for family and community.

Live to a personal code

Implementing a samurai-inspired personal 'code' (really just your values, ethics and morals) into your life will drive your habits and routines and lead to more productive and meaningful experiences. Make a list of values that you hold dear. What does *your* samurai code look like? It might include things like honesty, loyalty, respect, kindness, a robust work ethic, punctuality, avoiding wasteful consumption, or honouring the Earth. Think deeply on the values you wish to embody, commit them to memory and put them into practice every single day.

Practise compassion – towards yourself and others

Being compassionate is simpler than you might think. It's more than acts of kindness or charity; it's a condition of the heart. By being sympathetic to the distress and suffering of others – and ourselves – we strengthen those bonds and are more likely to extend love and generosity. It's also one of the best ways to boost our mental health and sense of wellbeing. It's easy to abandon compassion, especially when we're stressed at home or at work, or when the headlines get too loud. But with practice, we *can* reconnect with our heart. Being compassionate doesn't cost a thing – it's an immaterial gift – and it leads to healing, in ourselves and in the world around us.

Compassion allows us to take a break from the pursuit of our individual goals and objectives. Our attention is brought to bear on the essentials in life – the things that bring us deepest happiness. The samurai were more than just warriors; in addition to bravery and honour, compassion was central to their teachings.

Practise mindfulness

To become more compassionate, we must also practise mindfulness, cultivate our self-awareness and an awareness of others. When we're present, in the moment, and alert to our thoughts and emotions, we limit the distractions that stop us from being compassionate. We recognise but don't hold on to negative emotions. We are led by an inner voice that is supportive, gentle and accepting of all our experiences. By paying attention to our own thoughts, we are better able to understand the thoughts, emotions and actions of others, leading to greater empathy.

Practise gratitude and kindness

Being mindful of the people around us and recognising the things we are grateful for also benefits others. When we practise gratitude and kindness in front of our kids, for example, we teach them how to live with a positive attitude and a generous heart.

Be open-minded and let go of judgement

We never *really* know what's going on in other people's lives. When we judge them, we hamper our ability to empathise. It becomes harder to understand and honour their perspective. Instead, take a step back and try to imagine being in someone else's shoes – even just for a day. Everyone has shortcomings, and just because you might not understand them at first doesn't mean that they are irrelevant. This sort of mature, informed perspective leads to more meaningful relationships.

Be responsible for your actions

The act of taking responsibility for our actions – good, bad and indifferent – is a demonstration of self-compassion. It's also very wise! When we acknowledge our own mistakes and seek forgiveness, we are more inclined to extend forgiveness to others.

It is essential to look within and reflect on our actions and how they may have affected others. By accepting our flaws we can look at ways to better ourselves. We also become examples of integrity and honour.

Be fully present

Being fully present in mind, heart and spirit when connecting with other people enables us to be more empathetic and compassionate. When we shut out the distractions of the world around us and are fully in the moment, we are better able to listen deeply and understand other people's perspectives. By *truly* hearing others and connecting with their experiences – through the words they choose, their tone, emotions and body language – we foster deeper relationships, rather than just relying on what our initial assumptions and biases tell us. Showing up fully present validates others' experiences and emotions; we are signalling that we *see them*, *hear them* and *care about them*.

THE ART OF SELF-CONTROL

Most of us find it impossible to delay gratification. It's just so hard to do! Ultimately, we alone are responsible for our attitudes, and those attitudes shape our decisions and the way we interact with others – for better and for worse. We all run the risk of losing so much of ourselves with the stresses and frantic pace of modern life and our endless pursuit of convenience. We are losing touch with our bodies and minds, and this results in damage to ourselves and our environment. Sadly, I see this in my clients every day.

That's why self-control – our ability to regulate our behaviours and impulses – is such a crucial aspect of health and longevity. Self-control helps us to resist those everyday temptations and delay gratification; it steers us towards healthier, more informed choices. Self-control involves *consciously* regulating our thoughts, emotions and actions in the face of conflicting desires or impulses. Most encouragingly, self-control is a skill that can be learned – and improved with regular practice. We *can* win the tug-of-war between where our first impulses are leading us and those healthier, long-term ambitions we have for ourselves.

The benefits of self-control

Exercising self-control helps manage stress, reduces certain health risk factors, improves relationships, and keeps us on the path towards our goals. Research has shown that individuals with high levels of self-control have better overall health and a longer life expectancy. They are also less likely to engage in risky behaviours, such as smoking, or alcohol and drug misuse.

Developing self-control requires intention and effort. Here are some techniques you can put into practice today:

- **Self-awareness:** focus on your initial thoughts and emotions when you are faced with unhealthy choices and temptations. Recognise that they are only impulses until they're acted on.
- **Healthy distractions:** you can short-circuit the impulse to make unhealthy decisions by engaging in healthy activities or shifting your focus to another goal. Instead of grabbing

a beer and a takeaway menu after work, for example, lace up your shoes and go for a short run. Even a sunset walk is better than beers, TV and takeaway!

- **Delayed gratification:** practising self-control doesn't mean draining all pleasure from your life. We're *postponing* gratification – and redefining what gratification means – by developing a long-term, healthy vision for our life. True rewards are different from those that come with immediate pleasure. (Most of us – me included – learned this the hard way!)

- **Self-reward:** celebrate the small wins and reward yourself when you make progress towards your bigger goals. An ice-cream tastes that little bit sweeter when you've shaved minutes off your PB or had a long session training with your mates at the surf club.

- **Mindfulness:** practise the mindfulness, meditation and deep breathing techniques we discussed in Chapters 5 and 6 when you feel the urge to break the healthy routines you've put in place. They will quickly bring you back into focus.

Common obstacles to practising self-control

Self-control is not instinctive and it is not permanent. You have to work at it! Here are some of the factors that can challenge our self-control – and our longevity – and require us to implement the disciplines we've put in place to keep us on track.

- **Stress** can compromise our self-control by distracting our minds and triggering our 'fight or flight' response. To limit the effects of stress, exercise to burn off the negative energy, and meditate to recentre yourself. Reach out to supportive friends and family. Be open and honest about whatever is getting you down. Compassion is a two-way street.

- **Fatigue** really affects our self-control. It's hard to rely on your willpower when you've flogged yourself at work and have nothing left in the tank. To overcome fatigue, prioritise sleep, hydrate with quality water, exercise regularly and stick to your healthy nutrition plan. A replenished mind and body will steer you towards better decision-making.

- **Temptation** has been shaping human history for aeons! And it all starts with our first impulses. Sometimes temptation can feel impossible to resist and we wave the white flag before self-control has had a chance to kick in. But if we recognise our triggers, we limit our exposure to them, and we allow ourselves to have a bit of space between thought and action. As a result, the next decision we make is more likely to be a healthy one.

THE POWER OF CHANGE OVER THE LONG HAUL

Finding the motivation to make positive changes is hard. No two ways about it. You are not alone in feeling this. It can often seem overwhelming, especially when the results aren't immediate. Being mindful of how we think and feel during difficult times is crucial. We need to learn patience and persistence and understand we're in it for the long haul. Taking breaks, practising self-care and surrounding ourselves with supportive people are all beneficial in making positive life changes lasting ones.

The samurai trained persistently in martial arts for years to prepare their bodies and minds for battle. They understood how important it was to stick to their code and practices every single day. They would stop to rest and recover, but their mission, their vigilance, never wavered. They kept honing their physical skills and putting their minds and spirit to work in support of the cause of compassion. They never ceased living a life of honour.

In today's fast-paced world, it's easy to get caught up and forget that we're in it for the long haul. We become consumed with quick wins – sugar fixes – that don't last. We obsess over just putting one foot in front of the other, on the minutiae. We focus on just getting by today.

This is why the pursuit of longevity really is an art. This is why I place such emphasis on routine and discipline, focus and vision. Those are the elements needed to see lasting change across our lives. We must learn from our past mistakes and understand that failure is part of the journey. Only then are we able to approach the future with maturity and openness. We find the bravery needed to recognise when something is working in our lives – or holding us back – and when further changes are needed. We need to adapt to the environment that is constantly changing around us.

Remember to stay positive! Take a step back occasionally and assess your life from a different perspective. Appreciate how far you've come and get ready for the rest of the journey.

Understand when you need to take a break and recharge so you can come back stronger. If I have a year that's particularly taxing, I'll take a week's break every three months or so to regain my balance and re-energise myself. Sometimes I might even take a day off work just to spend quality time with my family and loved ones. Whatever helps you find the motivation and strength to stay motivated for the long haul, embrace and explore it.

As we end this part of the journey together, let's remind ourselves of the main things we need to keep in mind in our pursuit of a lifetime of longevity and wellness.

Be patient

You cannot achieve lasting greatness overnight. Don't believe in the magic pills people are trying to sell you. Results and success take time, patience and persistence. Being patient in this day and age can be considered an art too! Remember, every step you're taking now, in this moment, is one more in the direction of your goal of a long, fulfilling life. Stay on the path. Embrace the challenge.

Be driven by purpose

Envision what you want to accomplish and go after it with fire and froth in your belly. It's essential. A sense of 'why' will get you through the tough times. Experiment until you find your passion – the things that fuel and fulfil you. Life's challenges will always be there – but so will you.

Embrace the journey!

Life is busy, beautiful, drama-filled and full of mysteries. The journey is more significant than we think; we must trust and enjoy the process. Take time to marvel at how far you've come, the lessons learned along the way, and the people who have surrounded you (and are yet to come). Live with a big heart and big gratitude.

Learn and adapt when you need to

We've built flexibility and movement into your daily routine, so be flexible and agile in your mindset throughout your life. Be curious, learn, adapt, and be open to new experiences. Life is full of changes and challenges. Some obstacles will always be there, and you can't control everything. But you *can* control how you respond.

Consistency is key

Maintaining healthy routines can be the difference between success and failure. Some days it will feel effortless and invigorating. Other days it will feel like hard work, and your fire is nowhere to be found. When you feel this way, persist in your daily routines to create the momentum (and results) you need to carry you through the rough patches. Remember, what you do *every day* matters far more than what you do *occasionally*.

So take your time. Enjoy the ride. There's so much ahead of you.

ACKNOWLEDGEMENTS

Thank you to my publisher and editor, Brandon, for motivating me and giving me this massive opportunity – it's a dream come true. I am so happy and grateful.

Thank you to the entire Holistic HQ crew for supporting and understanding my time away from the clinic.

Thank you to my family – love you all!

Thank you to Tom Carroll, for the inspiration, motivation and guidance. Love you, Tom.

To learn more about my methodology and how to apply the exercises in this book and expand on them, please follow:

@holisticprohealth @theartoflongevity

Holistic Pro Health Performance

www.holisticph.com

Gratitude to all, Rodrigo B. Perez

Powered by Penguin

Looking for more great reads, exclusive content and book giveaways?

Subscribe to our weekly newsletter.

Scan the QR code or visit penguin.com.au/signup